Using Action Inquiry in Engaged Research

Additional titles in the Engaged Research and Practice for Social Justice in Education series:

Research, Actionable Knowledge, and Social Change
Reclaiming Social Responsibility Through Research Partnerships

Edward P. St. John
Foreword by Penny A. Pasque

Reflection in Action
A Guidebook for Student Affairs Professionals and Teaching Faculty

Kimberly A. Kline
Foreword by Edward P. St. John

Intersectionality in Educational Research

Edited by Dannielle Joy Davis, Rachelle J. Brunn-Bevel, and James L. Olive
Foreword by Susan R. Jones

Engaged Research and Practice
Higher Education and the Pursuit of the Public Good

Edited by Betty Overton, Penny A. Pasque, and John C. Burkhardt
Foreword by Tony Chambers
Series Foreword by Edward P. St. John

Using Action Inquiry in Engaged Research

An Organizing Guide

Edward P. St. John, Kim Callahan Lijana, and Glenda D. Musoba

Foreword by Timothy K. Eatman

Afterword by Rick Dalton

Sty/us

STERLING, VIRGINIA

Stylus

COPYRIGHT © 2017 BY
STYLUS PUBLISHING, LLC.

Published by Stylus Publishing, LLC.
22883 Quicksilver Drive
Sterling, Virginia 20166-2102

All rights reserved. No part of this book may be reprinted or reproduced in any form or by any electronic, mechanical, or other means, now known or hereafter invented, including photocopying, recording, and information storage and retrieval, without permission in writing from the publisher.

Library of Congress Cataloging-in-Publication Data
The CIP data for this title has been applied for.

13-digit ISBN: 978-1-57922-834-7 (cloth)
13-digit ISBN: 978 1 57922-835-4 (paper)
13-digit ISBN: 978 1 57922-836-1 (library networkable e-edition)
13-digit ISBN: 978 1 57922-837-8 (consumer e-edition)

Printed in the United States of America

All first editions printed on acid-free paper
that meets the American National Standards Institute
Z39-48 Standard.

> Bulk Purchases
>
> Quantity discounts are available for use in workshops and for staff development.
> Call 1-800-232-0223

First Edition, 2017

10 9 8 7 6 5 4 3 2 1

CONTENTS

Tables — *vii*

Figures — *ix*

Foreword — *xi*
 Timothy K. Eatman

Acknowledgments — *xv*

Introduction — *1*

1. Getting Started — *4*
2. Focus on Barriers to Social Justice — *18*
3. Organizing for Change — *41*
4. Using Information for Change — *69*
5. Learning From Experience — *119*

Afterword — *129*
 Rick Dalton

References — *133*

About the Contributors — *135*

Index — *139*

TABLES

Table 2.1 CFES Reporting Instruments in Relation to Evaluation Criteria	*33*
Table 2.2 Average ACT Composite Score for the 11th Grade by School Type: 2007 and 2010	*39*
Table 3.1 Alignment of CFES Core Practices and the Social Processes Related to Academic Capital Formation	*61*
Table 4.1 Role of Research and Evaluation in Action Inquiry	*76*
Table 4.2 DC TAG Graduates After Four, Five, and Six Years by High School Type	*82*
Table 4.3 DC TAG Graduates After Four, Five, and Six Years by Type of First College Attended	*84*
Table 4.4 2003–2005 Cohort Graduation Rate Comparison at Most Attended Colleges	*86*
Table 4.5 Grade Levels of Green and All CFES Respondents	*91*
Table 4.6 Students Reporting Participation in Federal Free and Reduced Cost Lunch at Green Compared to All CFES Respondents	*91*
Table 4.7 Race/Ethnicity of Green Students Compared to All CFES Respondents	*92*
Table 4.8 Highest Education Levels of Students' Families for Green Students Compared to All CFES Students	*92*

Table 4.9 CFES Scholars Engagement in College/Career Pathways Practices for Green Students Compared to All CFES Respondents — *93*

Table 4.10 Green Students' Plans After High School Compared to All CFES Respondents — *94*

Table 4.11 CFES Scholar Engagement in Mentoring and Social Support for Green Students Compared to All CFES Respondents — *95*

Table 4.12 Student Involvement in Engaged Leadership Practices Comparing Green and All CFES Respondents — *96*

Table 4.13 Items Cited by Teachers as Sources and Targets of Issues — *112*

FIGURES

Figure 1.1. Framing actionable theories of college preparation, access, and success. *8*

Figure 1.2. Case studies illustrating engaged research projects supporting interventions promoting equity in higher education. *16*

Figure 3.1. Role of preliminary evaluation in the action inquiry cycle: The short loop through inquiry. *45*

Figure 4.1. Percentage of DC TAG grantees whose gender is male, female, or unknown. *80*

Figure 4.2. Cumulative graduation rate (%) of the 2003, 2004, and 2005 DC TAG cohorts. *80*

FOREWORD

The current era of widespread access to information on demand, while enigmatic and seductive, is complicated by a pervasive and unprecedented societal interrogation of the once dominant "expert knows best" model of knowledge-making and consumption. We are witnessing a pointed rejection of "the establishment" (and derision of the status quo in general) which some argue may be most powerfully represented in the 2016 U.S. presidential campaign and election. Key among the many lessons that pundits, pollsters, politicians, and people of all walks of life have come to understand in a new way from these developments is the fact that all information is not created equal. Truly, this glaring variance among knowledge sources and questions about information integrity requires special attention and carries profound social implications.

Given the advent of social media, we see the proliferation of information sources, inadequately vetted but nonetheless used to illuminate and analyze consequential social matters. Many of these matters reveal and reflect the persistent wounds of inequality, grossly undertreated and festering within our society. In this environment, how are our understandings about the principles of knowledge-making and use evolving? What lessons are there to be learned about the work of research and knowledge generation within institutions of higher education? How can extensive stores of knowledge and systems of knowledge production be used to mitigate social injustice? To what extent can we look to scholarship as a means of supporting and activating this American experiment in democracy?

St. John, Lijana, and Musoba, authors of *Using Action Inquiry in Engaged Research: An Organizing Guide,* have produced a volume that addresses these questions by pivoting on the efficacy of engaged scholarship. They propose action inquiry as a framework to reconceptualize and expand the continuum of knowledge creation for the university of the twenty-first century. It is true that many still regard higher education as a nerve center of intellectual and social enlightenment. And there are arguably as many others who maintain that the ivory tower has fallen short of its purposes and should be "leveled"; I am not certain that I totally disagree with this view. Of course, this places me in a bit of an awkward position as a university professor and researcher. However, my sense is that such a leveling would be useful, even transformative, if advanced toward the purpose of making more even, or making a stronger case for expanding our understandings about what constitutes knowledge rather than doing away with or demolishing prevailing traditional notions of scholarship. In this book, St. John and his colleagues enact such a leveling of sorts by specifying more robust ways to generate and use knowledge for social amelioration especially through educational research.

While academic training and degree pursuits classify me as an educational sociologist, I am equally proud to traverse my work in academe as a publicly engaged scholar. My position as faculty codirector of Imagining America: Artists and Scholars in Public Life (IA), a national consortium of more than 100 higher education institutions and community-based partners working at the nexus of the cultural disciplines (humanities, arts, and design) and community engagement greatly nourishes this identity. I am compelled by the approaches and strategies of action inquiry in engaged research as much of my energy, work and leadership with IA focuses on questions of the epistemology of knowledge making. Significant aspects of our work address faculty roles and rewards, the emerging citizenry of academe, full participation, and perhaps most important of all, positive cultural change within the academy. This volume speaks to these domains fittingly characterized as issues of "scholarship in action," in the words of social psychologist and university chancellor Nancy Cantor.

Using Action Inquiry in Engaged Research: An Organizing Guide, employs informationally rich and pedagogically intriguing strategies that are difficult to operationalize in book format. For me, it reads in part like a synthesized collection of professional development modules. For example, with respect to structure, the chapters, each accompanied by literal guidances, signal the intentionality of the book. If readers are like me, they will find themselves rolling up their sleeves while gleaning from its insights. Ten pregnant case studies dispersed throughout evoke a dynamic praxis very useful for workshops and strategic planning

Among the many refreshments of this project, I experience the authors as advancing efforts to level the ivory tower by making skillful use of leveling language and concepts which extend from studied theoretical perspectives grounded in extant literature. Constructs like forming academic capital, developing an actionable theory of change, and interrogating a "lockstep theory of student progress with standardized requirements for each transition" (p. 21, this volume) to offer a few examples, represent the authors' desire to rupture the entrenched dysfunctions that all too often display overripened academic research withering on knowledge vines accessible only to "the learned few." This leveling language exposes in some cases an almost wholesale spoiling of knowledge due to the lack of a full complement of nutrients which should include intellectual and practical considerations both from outside and inside the academy. To be sure, this approach calls for leveling language and action that lead to the development of actionable theories followed by thoughtful cycles of theory, revision, and action.

These authors are unapologetic about using leveling language and articulating honest practices including reflections on stalled initiatives. One example is found in the case of the Detroit Public schools where a seemingly simple effort to secure data unfolded in a protracted way, damaging the health and life of the research project. Case studies, many presented in story format with detailed reflections, and analyses from a range of perspectives (e.g., community partners, researchers, graduate students) interspersed throughout, add a complexity to the guide that readers who demand varying perspectives on project evaluation will appreciate. In addition, readers who are dedicated to transformative change in educational research are treated to bursts of specific suggestions for practice and challenged with critical questions for discussion useful for strategic planning outlined within each chapter.

The importance of this book, the scope of work, and the approaches to knowledge-making that it represents has increased for me as I navigate a career transition from IA faculty codirector to a new role as inaugural dean of the Honors Living Learning Community (HLLC) at Rutgers University–Newark. We endeavor through the HLLC to establish an expansive model of honors programs that levels the status quo in the same spirit of the ivory tower leveling proposed earlier in this foreword; a model that seeks to give voice and place among the ranks of honors students to those who have traditionally been overlooked for participation in such programs. This paradigm shift requires that we develop a new way of looking at what is before us, acknowledging the blind spots and having the effrontery to interrupt the normative rhythm of ivory tower practices. In like manner, the authors of this book assert and demonstrate the expediency of drawing on strategies and methodologies employed by community organizers, for example, or the creation and acknowledgement and integration of more expansive scholarly artifacts into the coin of the realm. It may urge innovative processes with data generation and handling as in the migration of legacy data systems described in the chapters.

The cases demonstrate how interrogation of education systems and social inequality informs "research-informed advocacy for educational and social justices" (p. 119, this volume). They provide thoughtful approaches for using action inquiry to bring a learning orientation to educational reform. For example, the story about the organizational history and evolution of the Foundation for Excellent Schools changing its name to College For Every Student (CFES) recounted by Rick Dalton embodies the deep theory of change-driven work that can lead to transformation. The collaborations presented and reflected upon demonstrate the essential nature of reciprocity as well as the challenges and costs of placing a deliberate focus on equity in educational research. These cases also illustrate how CFES's practices of mentoring, pathways to college, and leadership through service promote uplift for underrepresented students.

Timothy K. Eatman
Dean, Honors Living Learning Community
Rutgers University–Newark
Faculty Codirector, Imagining America: Artists and Scholars in Public Life

ACKNOWLEDGMENTS

In projects using research to inform initiatives promoting social justice we found that (a) action inquiry should be integrated into decisions in practice and policy and (b) engaged research designed to inform these processes presents university-based researchers with new opportunities. The Ford Foundation and College For Every Student (CFES) funded projects used to test the action inquiry model within school-college partnerships. These projects included assessment research, development and analysis of case studies, workshops supporting interventions, and evaluation studies that have been adapted as reflective exercises in the steps to finding solutions to ongoing problems. Greg Anderson, Fred Frelow, and Jeannie Oakes were project officers at the Ford Foundation, which provided grants that informed the development of six cases. Rick Dalton (CFES chief operating officer) became a research partner and provided funding for projects resulting in three cases. We gratefully acknowledge this financial support. The ideas and interpretations presented in this book are the authors' and not intended to represent policies or positions of funding organizations, except as noted by funding authors from these agencies.

Graduate students and project staff contributed to the development and testing of the action inquiry model summarized in this guidebook, including Max Altman, Adam Baker, Hamida Bhagirathy-Bastin, Victoria Milazzo Bigelow, Anna Chiang, Nate Daun-Barnett, Amy S. Fisher, Feven Girmay, Kelicia Hollis, Stacy Jacob, Leanne Kang, Malisa Lee, Ashley Legitime, Johanna Masse, Cindy Veenstra, and Krystal Williams; some of these researchers are coauthors of the case studies generated by their research. Phyllis Kreger Stillman provided editorial support for development of this guide.

Support from colleagues also helped with the action projects summarized in this guide. John B. Williams (University of Maryland) and William T. Trent (University of Illinois) were coprincipal investigators on the planning grant for Projects Promoting Equity in Urban and Higher

Education, an initiative at the University of Michigan's National Center for Institutional Diversity (NCID). At the University of Michigan (UM), Phil Bowman (founding director of NCID) and Nick Collins (founding director of the Center for Educational Outreach) were advisers throughout the development of these projects. We deeply appreciate this support.

INTRODUCTION

Action inquiry provides a means for designing and evaluating intervention in education systems and practices to promote equity. *Engaged scholarship* is a strategy that educators, administrators, and students can use in partnerships with researchers to build knowledge and skills to support and inform the change process. We provide guidance and case studies to illustrate straightforward practices for building empowering partnerships. We also provide guidance by explaining how lessons learned from working with communities and schools can inform engaged scholarship on a broad range of projects addressing social injustices.

Getting Started

- *Develop a preliminary actionable theory.* An actionable theory is one that can be tested though an intervention. Clearly lay out how you expect an intervention to influence students' educational transitions (your propositions) and the information you need to test these propositions.
- *Find thought partners committed to empowering students.* Thought partners reflect together about barriers facing students and organizational practices that could empower students by encouraging them to find pathways congruent with their aspirations.
- *Learn from experience working with students.* Taking a student-centered approach to change in educational systems provides exciting opportunities for our own personal growth and learning, along with the satisfaction of helping others navigate their pathways to academic success.

Focus on Barriers to Social Justice

- *Identify barriers* facing the students you serve that might be reduced through interventions you can help organize.
- *Locate information sources* that can inform intervention strategies, including information routinely collected by the educational systems with which you work.
- *Analyze challenges* using data and information from existing sources to identify possible remedies.

Organize for Change

- *Define interventions that could empower students to navigate educational systems and explore opportunities.* Too frequently educational systems discourage students. Pay attention to patterns of departure and dropout to identify points where encouragement and assistance are needed.
- *Design projects to inform practice.* Educators are often wary of research because of the burdensome nature of public accountability systems, while researchers are often steeped in tautological theories that are true but essentially useless in promoting change
- *Start with interventions utilizing available resources.* When interventions depend on new funding to get started, they may never get going, so focus on interventions that can be designed using current funding. To make it easier to evaluate outcomes of an intervention, change agents within organizations should consult with potential research partners during the start-up process to include evaluation as part of intervention design.

Use Information for Change

- *Review your organization's formal and informal decision-making processes to identify when research can be used to inform actions to promote equity.* Educational organizations have formal planning, budgeting, and accountability processes, but these entities typically do not reinforce efforts to reduce inequality or shrink gaps in opportunity and achievement for underrepresented students.

- *Investigate the student data available.* Information technology makes it easier to collect student tracking data, which can then be analyzed as part of action inquiry to inform intervention design.
- *Reflect on when and how student surveys might inform decisions about policy and practice.* Surveys provide a sound, proven, and economical approach for examining student engagement in interventions, but developing a new questionnaire takes time.
- *Consider when independent research assistance would be helpful.* Interviews and focus groups can capture students' perspectives and provide a means of gaining insights that inform practice and can be used for advocacy to expand opportunity. Partnerships with researchers can provide a means of conducting this type of research in a professional and publishable manner.
- *Consider practitioners' perspectives when designing, implementing, testing, and refining intervention strategies.* To secure the authentic voices of educators engaged in implementing reforms, it is essential to ensure anonymity so they won't experience retribution for their critiques. This is an essential part of the process of securing permission and ensuring human subjects' protection. Partnerships with researchers will streamline this process.

Learn From Experience

Building expertise for breaking barriers involves reflecting on and learning from experience. As a conclusion, we reflect briefly on our experience working within K–12 and higher education to expand and improve educational opportunities for underrepresented students. We encourage readers to join in this process.

This guide is written for practitioners in schools, colleges, and community-based organizations. Discussion of cases studies as examples can help researchers and practitioners engage in projects that use action inquiry and research evidence to inform strategies for change.

1

GETTING STARTED

> **Guidance 1: Getting Started**
>
> 1. *Identify emerging challenges*: While systems and procedures are used in public and private organizations to improve quality, minimize errors, and achieve efficiency, the process invariably creates problems for individuals, groups, species, and/or environments. This book addresses challenges emerging from the transition to universal college preparation.
> 2. *Build partnerships to focus on promoting social justice*: Systemic reforms tend to benefit the overall population, but not low-income families. We focus on building partnerships that promote equity in high schools and colleges and support state and local initiatives to improve college preparation, access, equity in admissions, and persistence of low-income students.
> 3. *Use engaged scholarship to identify and test strategies for social action*: Changing systems requires building and testing social action within public and private organizations and within legal and policy constraints. This guide provides frameworks that can be used in 9–16 education and adapted to address other critical challenges undermining social justice.

The challenge of educational reform not only involves expanding college opportunities for students underrepresented among college graduates and the middle class (included in the broad term *underrepresented students*) but also requires communication with students and parents about educational and career opportunities. Increasingly, low-income students are from families with at least some college. Therefore schools, community-based organizations (CBOs), and colleges must rethink strategies for reducing gaps in educational attainment and economic opportunity.

Using *action inquiry*—defined as observations, reflections, and information from research—educators can identify and remedy barriers to success for these students. This guide provides flexible practices for integrating advocacy of underrepresented students into educational systems using evidence-based strategies. Each chapter introduces practices with a guide for action. The reflective case studies (found in chapters 2, 3, and 4) demonstrate the use of the action-inquiry cycle in bottom-up organizational change promoting the following:

- *Preparation*: Improving opportunities to prepare for college through quality education and social support
- *Access*: Transforming college outreach, admissions, and support services once in college to improve diversity in collegiate learning environments
- *College success*: Providing the academic, social, and financial support necessary to assure underrepresented students have fair opportunities for college completion

Advocates for underrepresented students and activist researchers share an interest in using their knowledge and skills to inform educational improvement. When interventions are based on what worked in another area, they usually must be adapted to address local challenges and constraints. We focus on the following three interrelated change processes essential to efforts to reduce gaps in preparation, access, and success:

1. *Overcoming barriers facing students:* Identify strategies that reduce inequality using reflection on experiences, reviews of research, and analysis of information provided by accountability systems.
2. *Organizing to support students' navigation of educational pathways:* Build partnerships to acquire information, and use research to inform improvements in practice and advocacy for students.
3. *Changing systems and practices to support underrepresented students:* Address barriers due to economic opportunities that undermine family and community support as well as institutionalized practices in education that reinforce and replicate inequality.

Student advocates in educational systems need information on how well their interventions actually work. Most educational systems have planning and accountability systems that provide data on outcomes but lack sound strategies for using this information to reduce inequality in outcomes. Student advocates working with underrepresented students must continually improve practices if schools and colleges are to succeed in reducing gaps.

Reflect on What Your Organization Can Do (Actionable Theory of Change)

Undergraduate and graduate programs in education and the social sciences provide information from theory, research, and practice, providing one basis for professional knowledge and skills. Since both society and professional knowledge change at a rapid pace, it is also crucial to reflect on practice, especially when considering remedies to educational inequality.

The growing income inequality in the United States provides a complicated and troubling context for education reforms that expect all students to prepare for college. Educators should rethink old assumptions about how poverty hinders educational opportunity. The goal of expanding and improving educational opportunity through college preparation for all students is implicit in the Common Core State Standards (CCSS). The theory of change used by CCSS in high schools (i.e., the evidence-based standards) assumes that pedagogies that previously worked for students to prepare them socially and educationally for advanced courses will continue to work under the new guidelines. But wealth disparities also affect achievement in required courses, college access, college success, and navigation of educational and career pathways.

Student debt has become a serious problem for middle- and low-income families. For more than two decades, low-income students in college have had to work long hours as well as borrow excessively to pay for college, conditions that substantially extend their time to degrees. The net costs of college after need-based grants for low-income students are higher than at any point in history. Some parents of low-income students have attended college but did not receive the expected benefits.

The notion that raising high school graduation requirements will equalize educational and economic opportunity for all students is a deceptive myth for some underrepresented students. This myth has been especially harmful as it has taken shape in urban school systems and universities without acknowledgment of the high level of debt that may be required to attain a college degree in many states. Attempts to change students to fit a savagely unequal system have further accelerated disparities in many urban communities.

The core challenge is to adapt educational pathways to empower students to navigate this education system with insight about potential career pathways. Using an *actionable approach* to educational practice can help us focus on reducing the effect of institutionalized barriers to opportunity in the current educational system. This involves testing our assumptions about the practices (content, pedagogies, networking, financial support, etc.) that will improve opportunity.

We encourage readers to use action inquiry to examine current practices and try out new approaches for empowering students. We start with a framework you can use to develop an actionable theory of change for your own practice (Figure 1.1). *Consider your own assumptions and think about how your work might improve and expand educational opportunity for underrepresented students, focusing on the following student transitions:*

1. From middle school to a high school that fits students' interests and abilities, an especially difficult challenge for low-income students in urban school systems with competing magnet and charter schools
2. From high school to a college that is committed to their academic success, a process that requires attention to admissions, academic support, and transfer programs within colleges and universities
3. From introductory courses into a major program that matches emerging aspirations, recognizing that most students learn about additional educational options after they enter college, and that many change their major and/or transfer to another college

Reflect on your own actions using research evidence, personal observations, and insights from your knowledge of the education system. Think about your reflections in relation to the framework (Figure 1.1). To be actionable, your theory of change should identify an intervention that you can

8   USING ACTION INQUIRY IN ENGAGED RESEARCH

Figure 1.1. Framing actionable theories of college preparation, access, and success.

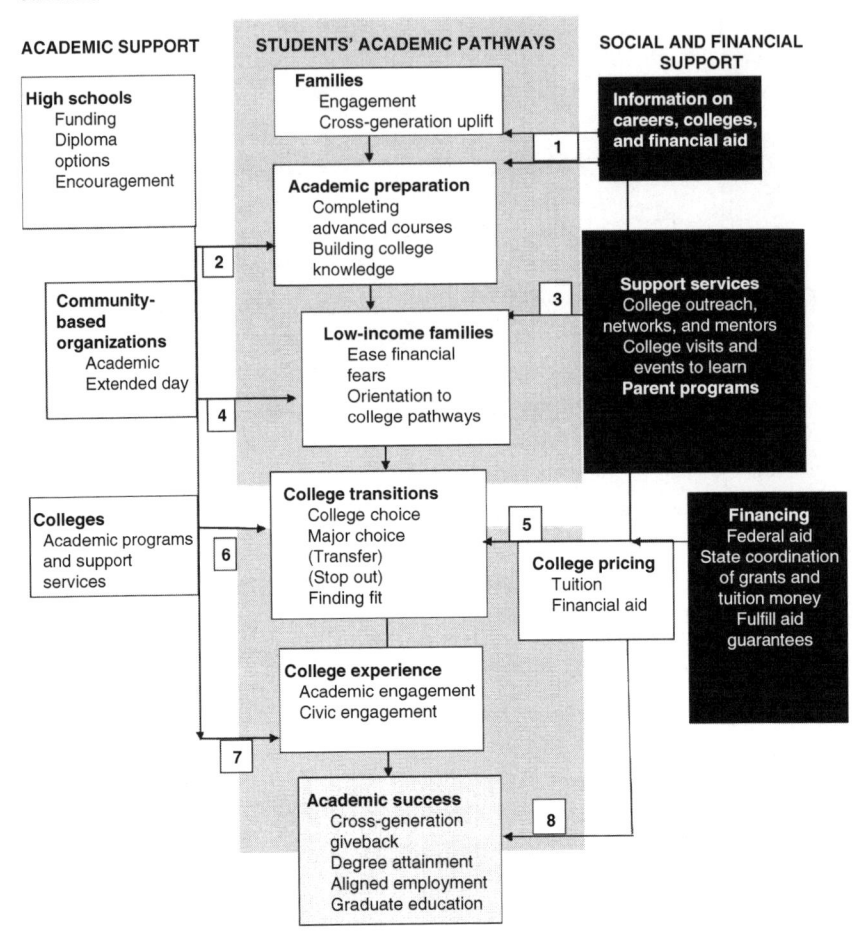

ACADEMIC SUPPORT	STUDENTS' ACADEMIC PATHWAYS	SOCIAL AND FINANCIAL SUPPORT
High schools Funding Diploma options Encouragement	**Families** Engagement Cross-generation uplift	**Information on careers, colleges, and financial aid**
	Academic preparation Completing advanced courses Building college knowledge	
Community-based organizations Academic Extended day	**Low-income families** Ease financial fears Orientation to college pathways	**Support services** College outreach, networks, and mentors College visits and events to learn **Parent programs**
Colleges Academic programs and support services	**College transitions** College choice Major choice (Transfer) (Stop out) Finding fit	**College pricing** Tuition Financial aid / **Financing** Federal aid State coordination of grants and tuition money Fulfill aid guarantees
	College experience Academic engagement Civic engagement	
	Academic success Cross-generation giveback Degree attainment Aligned employment Graduate education	

try out in your local context. Since state policies on education, local educational practices, school and college funding, student aid funding, and individual students' family cultures are highly variable, there is no single strategy that will overcome the effects of income inequality. In addition, strategies used to teach, provide support services, and finance educational choices vary across locales, and actionable theory must be adaptable to local circumstances.

> **Practice**
> **Identify strategies your organization can try out**
> **(Develop an actionable theory)**
>
> An actionable theory of change can be tested by an intervention. Explicate how you expect an intervention to influence students' transitions and educational outcomes and include a means of evaluating whether the intervention had the desired results.
>
> To prepare for action inquiry, reflect on the following ways you can use evidence to improve your practice in your current role:
>
> - *Review the linkages in the framework to identify action points.* How do the programs and services you are engaged in relate to the trajectories students follow to educational success?
> - *Hypothesize on how your actions can empower students to navigate toward their visions of academic and career success.* Think about what you do and could do to improve and expand equal opportunities for the students you serve.
> - *Use your hypotheses to reflect on practice and outcomes using available evidence.* Thinking about how your actions link to outcomes provides an opportunity to reflect on evidence from current practices and try out new practices.
> - *Identify additional evidence that would help inform decisions about alternative strategies.* Is there evidence generated by your institution that you have not used to inform your decisions and those of the organization? Should you review the existing research? Is new research needed?

Partners for Student-Centered Approaches to Organizing

A local, actionable theory of change should consider how federal, state, and local policies constrain or encourage student opportunities and how interventions influence student trajectories through educational and social systems, including transitions among systems (gaining access, transferring, changing content specialization, etc.). Low-income students face barriers because of differences in resources and support systems. To improve fairness, it may be necessary to intervene to accomplish the following:

- Change current practices to empower students' navigation of systemic barriers
- Develop new intervention strategies that can change systemic barriers
- Restructure existing policies and programs to overcome systemic inequalities

Networks Can Support Student Success

Reflection on how our assumptions and experiences inform actionable theories of change and evidence informs the construction and reconstruction of intervention strategies. When framing your actionable theory of change, think about how the intervention actually links to educational transitions. Consider the following examples, referring to the framework in Figure 1.1:

- Family engagement in education (e.g., choosing schools, supporting children) is a crucial aspect of educational preparation. Students whose parents have degrees from four-year colleges have inherent advantages in preparation compared to prospective first-generation college students. In addition, parents' concerns about college costs can limit their engagement. Interventions in families can influence early choices about education (linkage 1) but are also possible in subsequent educational transitions (e.g., student and family support services).
- Most states have adopted new graduation requirements using the theoretical assumption that courses completed will influence eventual success (linkage 2). These policies assume improved preparation opens up pathways to college and eventual degree completion for students from underrepresented groups.
- College access organizations, including school-college networks like College For Every Student (CFES), provide support services that introduce underrepresented students to college and career pathways (linkage 3). These networks test assumptions about how social support can empower students and help develop the college knowledge they would not otherwise have.

- Many community organizations and reformers seek to intervene directly to improve academic preparation (linkage 4).
- The strategies colleges use to provide aid to students to supplement federal and state grant and loan programs influence whether students can afford to pay for college (linkage 5) and attain a degree (linkage 8). Student navigation of college costs, including the extent of borrowing and work, also influences their eventual commitment to give back to their colleges and future generations (linkage 8).
- Academic programs and student services in college have direct links to access (linkage 6), college engagement (linkage 7), and eventual college success.

Using evidence to think critically about how these linkages work locally in students' lives provides valuable information about barriers, opportunities, and strategies students use to navigate around barriers to actualize opportunities for academic success. Local educators and community-based advocates often have a tacit theory of change with an implicit logic about how their intervention will empower students. The evidence they accumulate to document pathways students actually travel, along with insights (positions) about how they traverse through and around barriers, provides crucial actionable information for practice.

There are many resources that schools, community organizations, and colleges can use to form partnerships to address challenges related to counseling, student aid, and sociocultural support, finding financial aid, and learning about college and career pathways (Dalton & St. John, 2016). We encourage new partnerships to use data to build the case for funding from external sources—community, corporate, and national foundations, along with state and federal grant programs—that share their commitment to expanding educational opportunity.

When building partnerships, share understandings of actionable theories of change. Articulating and testing assumptions about change—sharing information about barriers and opportunities to address them—inform the development of actionable strategies. Build a collective understanding of the ways interventions link to—and potentially reduce—locally institutionalized inequalities in educational opportunity. Local changes in practice cannot change public policy but can adapt to policy constraints through innovation. In chapters 2, 3, and 4 we provide guidance and case studies to inform the development of local actionable theories of change. We structure those chapters to encourage reflections and conversations about local, actionable theories of change.

> **Practice**
> **Find thought partners**
>
> Thought partners reflect together about barriers facing students and organizational practices that could empower students by encouraging them to find pathways congruent with their aspirations. When leaders encourage reflection, it is often possible to develop *communities of practice*, defined as groups of practitioners who work together to expand and improve opportunity. It is usually possible to form networks or informal groups to help students learn how to navigate educational and social systems.
>
> 1. *Focus on the trajectories of the students you serve.* Consider how the students you work with make educational transitions. Talk with students about prior experiences, along with the challenges they face. In addition to your work, consider how others influence students as they strive for academic success and who might encourage them (i.e., potential mentors).
> 2. *Identify possible support networks.* Student support networks comprise formal systems in educational organizations, community groups, and families. Some students have good support networks, but others don't. Find out who else supports the students you serve and what they do and don't do.
> 3. *Think critically about the gaps in your students' support networks.* Think about others to consult when students face challenges. Learn from talking with students and reading reports from within the system about successful support.
> 4. *Form informal partnerships with people and organizations that actually can and do empower the students you serve.* It is possible to organize people to support students as they navigate through barriers. Find an affinity group (people you can trust) to support students and share with them evidence and experiences from intervention strategies.

Reflect on Alternatives With Prospective Partners

Actionable knowledge combines reflections on experiences, understandings of the ways research can inform action, and lessons learned from testing interventions in practice. Regardless of whether your educational system makes a concerted effort to support your innovation through bottom-up action inquiry and change, educators in schools and colleges and advocates in CBOs can engage in social and educational problem-solving to address the learning and social support needs of the students with whom they work. CBOs can encourage students by introducing them to college opportunities, providing social support through mentoring and encouraging them to engage in civic activities. Sharing information across partner organizations is needed to expand opportunity in the following ways:

- Alignment of high schools and community colleges
- Alignment of community colleges and four-year colleges
- Collaboration between universities and high school systems on pathway projects
- Support of community organizations for extended-day programs, internships, and service opportunities

Educational systems go through periods of rapid change as a consequence of changing policies, but such periods of change are usually followed by stable periods. When policies are stable and can be depended upon to provide a framework, it is possible to make changes in systems to really serve all students, making sure students have the resources to successfully navigate educational pathways. This is especially critical for students who are underrepresented among college graduates. In most urban education systems, there has been wave after wave of reform, creating systemic instability. Indeed, the rapid pace of policy change in the early years of the twenty-first century (e.g., new standards, rising graduation requirements, and use of market models for school reform) has turned reform into a constant, making it difficult for local educators to develop and test new practices. Justice advocates serving students in urban communities must be vigilant about using evidence to develop actionable strategies to support students.

> **Practice**
> **Share reflections on barriers facing students**
>
> Taking a student-centered approach to change in an educational system provides exciting opportunities for our own personal growth and learning as educators, along with the satisfaction of empowering others as they navigate pathways to academic success. Very often, having educators who supported us along the way helped inspire us to become educators and take on leadership roles in educational organizations. Remember, there is greater wealth inequality now in the United States than in the last half of the twentieth century, yet we expect students to achieve at higher levels than did past generations of students.
>
> 1. *Reflect on the ways financial and life circumstances influence students' experiences.* For those of us who made it through formal educational systems, it can be difficult to see the challenges facing low-income students and families in the early twenty-first century. Take a student-centered approach when thinking about your own professional practice.
> 2. *Think about opportunities to improve your practice and to collaborate with others to better serve underrepresented students.* U.S. education historically prepared only a minority of students for college; now all students are expected to complete a college preparatory curriculum. We need to do a better job of serving students who would not have tracked into this curriculum in the past.
> 3. *Learning new approaches to education requires a learning orientation among educational professionals.* While we should constantly learn from practices that have worked in the past, we also need to face the challenges we encounter as we serve today's students who are all traveling a pathway to college.

Learning From Case Studies

The cases in the next three chapters provide both research briefs prepared for school- and college-based partnerships and reflections on how the research was used to inform social justice advocacy. The cases are presented in temporal sequences, illustrating how researchers interacted with partners in educational and nonprofit organizations. Discussing the cases in groups provides opportunities to learn about how organizations use information, think critically about working with engaged scholars to build an evidence base to inform adaptive change, and also consider the limitations of action inquiry.

Case Method

The cases in this book are real and were written by social justice advocates and researchers who worked in partnerships. They illustrate that integrating an emphasis on equity into educational improvement is a frustrating and ongoing process. Even when innovations address challenges and remove barriers, which is not always the case, new problems emerge. The cases present evidence provided by researchers and the practitioners with whom they worked in their own voices. Figure 1.2 illustrates how the cases focus on improving equity in access and college success.

The cases were undertaken as part of Projects Promoting Equity in Higher and Urban Education, an initiative of the National Center for Institutional Diversity funded by a planning grant from the Ford Foundation. As part of this grant, we hosted a seminar on college access where Rick Dalton, chief executive officer of CFES, spoke; we also held a summit meeting as a means of assessing the nature of the challenges facing research partnerships in Washington, DC; Detroit, Michigan; and other cities. Three research partnerships evolved from these efforts: one in Washington, DC; one with CFES; and one with Detroit public schools. Within these partnerships, we moved through assessment and organizing and on to research informing local social justice advocates seeking to expand educational opportunity by improving college preparation, enrollment, and persistence. Using this inquiry-based sequence, researchers worked with partners in high schools, colleges, community networks, and state agencies.

The case studies are aligned with the practices for building partnerships that inform interventions to reduce barriers to college preparation,

Figure 1.2. Case studies illustrating engaged research projects supporting interventions promoting equity in higher education.

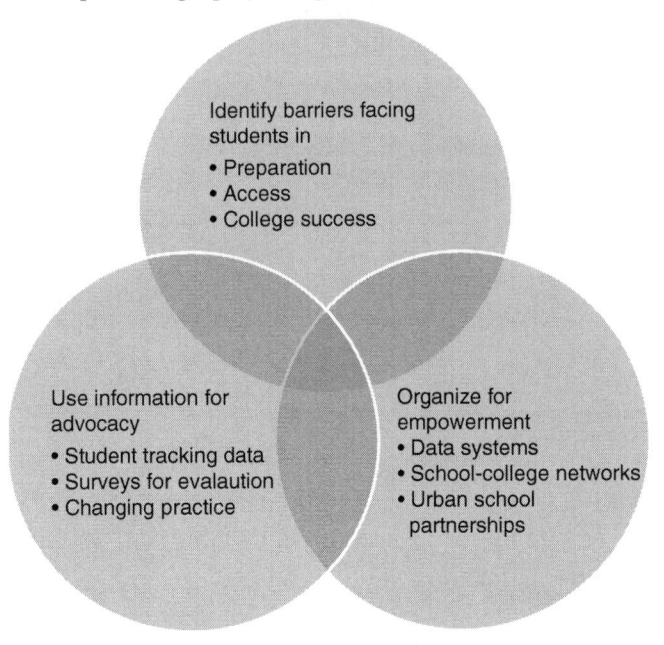

Identify barriers facing students in
- Preparation
- Access
- College success

Use information for advocacy
- Student tracking data
- Surveys for evalaution
- Changing practice

Organize for empowerment
- Data systems
- School-college networks
- Urban school partnerships

access, and success. *The cases are not intended as best practices.* Instead, readers can analyze the cases to see examples of testing actionable theories of change. We all need better information about what has and has not worked as intended. Readers can do the following:

- *Analyze the cases.* When reflecting on the cases, focus on your own learning by thinking about how you could develop research projects that address the challenges facing your practice. When working in small groups, discussion helps build shared actionable knowledge about potential change processes.
- *Reflect on your own experiences.* We provide questions after each case to encourage reflection on change strategies, embedded and explicit theories of change, and the strengths and limitations of intervention strategies (boxes at the end of cases). Discussing the

cases and sharing insights can encourage openness in discussing evidence in the ongoing improvement process.

By reflecting on the cases, community leaders, educators, and student activists can open up to learning from others' experiences, including the uses, misuses, and limitations of data and research. Using these practices can empower you as an agent of change.

2

FOCUS ON BARRIERS TO SOCIAL JUSTICE

Guidance 2: Focus on Barriers to Social Justice

1. *Identify barriers to social justice*: Social processes within communities, public and private organizations, and governing agencies can inadvertently conspire to reinforce inequality. Identifying barriers prospective students face is necessary before initiating reforms that seek to reduce inequalities created by formal and informal systems. We describe strategies used in 9–16 reforms.
2. *Start with information generated by systems*: Information on inequality is generally available as a result of formalized reporting and can be analyzed to test initial suppositions about embedded barriers to social justice. Engaged researchers and activists can assemble and analyze data to test propositions about barriers. We illustrate with case studies from engaged scholarship in partnerships formed to promote educational opportunities.
3. *Learn from experience*: Partnerships provide means for engaged scholars and change advocates to collaborate on initiatives promoting social justice. The case studies illustrate ways data were used to analyze challenges facing underrepresented groups.

The strategic planning and accountability schemes used by states, school districts, and colleges usually include some type of yearly data collection that informs annual plans and budgets. Unfortunately, government funding levels in public schools and colleges are seldom adequate to provide the services that can empower students (e.g., counselors), so educators compete for supplemental funding through grants or strategic initiatives. Diversity and equity issues usually are not addressed within funding formulas used in these budgeting models. Advocacy is essential. This chapter introduces practices that practitioners and working groups can use for evidence-based change. We also focus on aligning research with the process of identifying and testing intervention strategies. The guidance focuses on the following three necessary practices:

1. Identify barriers facing the students you serve that could be reduced through interventions you can organize;
2. Find sources of information that can help shape your intervention strategies, including information routinely collected by the educational system; and
3. Analyze challenges using data and information from existing sources to identify possible interventions.

The cases, drawn from actionable projects, address issues related to preparation and college transition as well as illustrate the process.

Guide for Action

Regardless of the methods used, frequent challenges surface in educational organizations because formal plans often do not align well with the realities of education. Typically, problems recur over time; either remedies do not work as intended or new, related problems emerge after alterations are made in the system (e.g., curriculum change, changes in student requirements).

Although many of the barriers facing underrepresented students are well documented in research, it can be difficult to see how the strategies used in organizations add to the barriers students face. Many critical challenges exist that create barriers to expanding and improving pathways to academic success for students underrepresented among college-educated professionals. To address these challenges, strategic initiatives should focus on remedying the *underlying problems*, defined as those structural, process, and social issues that undermine educational equity. Finding remedies to critical challenges can involve families, schools, community organizations, colleges and universities, and employers within the community—all of these groups are potential partners in strategic assessments.

Recurrent Challenges in Education Organizations

A large number of researchers have addressed the challenges facing schools and colleges as they change their practices to improve college preparation, broaden college access, and improve K–12 schools responsible for educating underrepresented students. Colleges, schools, and community organizations can build partnerships to focus on shared concerns, including the following:

- *Academic preparation for underrepresented students.* Transforming high schools so they can prepare their students for college remains a major challenge in most cities and rural communities. When schools fall short of standards, colleges and universities are faced with providing remedial or supplemental instruction as a means of ensuring diverse enrollment. Colleges and universities seeking to diversify their enrollment can

    o Examine the status of high school preparation in minority-serving schools and, when possible, identify potential partner schools
    o Partner on reform initiatives with these schools

- *9–14 transition and the community college system.* There is an increasing emphasis on raising the percentage of students who attain at least a two-year degree; in fact, many reform groups advocate making two-year degrees a minimum standard for all students. Barriers to the transition to a 9–14 system that can be addressed by partnerships include the following:

    o *Organizational:* Community college campuses are organizationally different from high schools and often not well aligned with transfer to four-year colleges;
    o *Financial:* High schools and community colleges have different funding mechanisms, and community college students have to pay tuition; and
    o *Social:* Many potential first-generation students do not learn enough about college options from counselors, family members, or other sources; those who do may not understand the different types of colleges.

- *Opportunities for transfer and change of major.* The theory of the educational pipeline as applied to science, technology, engineering, and math (STEM) fields has driven high school reform focusing on college preparation, the movement toward 9–14 education, and emphasis on math and science education in the early twenty-first century. Analyses of the movement of high school graduates into and through college consistently reveal similar challenges, such as the following:

- Many students who enter college in engineering and other STEM fields change their majors or drop out;
- Very few students who start out in non-STEM fields transfer into STEM majors; and
- Some STEM majors drop out or transfer instead of changing their major.

• *Form multiple pathways.* The pipeline model of education provides a lockstep theory of student progress with standardized requirements for each transition. This overlooks the many diverse ways students make choices and changes when circumstances turn out to be different than they had envisioned. Students change their minds as they learn more about themselves during high school and college. For example, to avoid excessive debt, many students work and attend college only periodically, when they can afford to do so and need to qualify for better jobs. Overemphasis on a rigid pipeline can divert attention from creating new pathways that promote academic success for working people who can benefit from additional courses and regional partnerships that support their continuous enrollment as they navigate work and education.

Organizing Information About Barriers and Possible Remedies

Most interventions that support underrepresented students are faced with the challenges of rationalizing their missions and finding and justifying funding. At a minimum, new ventures should consider the information that can inform their strategies: evidence related to local challenges, organizational theories of change, and the eventual evaluative evidence necessary to sustain funding. While schools, states, the federal government, and national organizations collect data on students, the reports produced from these sources typically do not provide information about the barriers facing students.

> **Practice**
> **Identify barriers facing underrepresented students**
>
> When we use student-centered views of educational trajectories, it is easier to see the barriers students face. Case 2.1 illustrates this early stage of developing partnerships.
>
> When building partnerships it is necessary to share information about challenges facing students as they make transitions. In meetings involving partners, consider the following questions:
>
> - What are the common barriers facing the students your organization serves or potentially can serve?
> - What strengths does your organization bring to a potential partnership?
> - What can your organization gain from partnering on intervention strategies?
> - What are the potential mutual benefits from developing a partnership to expand opportunities for underrepresented students?
> - What types of additional support (academic, organizational, social, and/or financial) would prospective students need to benefit from a partnership?
> - What kinds of information does your organization need to inform its decisions about investing in the partnership?
> - How might researchers inform the development of interventions as part of your partnership?

Focusing on Information Strategies

The best source of data for investigating student barriers and outcomes is student data tracked by educational systems over time—the points at which students depart the system and factors associated with departure (e.g., grades, moving). Increasingly, states and the federal government are investing in developing data systems that can be used for this purpose. For example, the Indiana Project on Academic Success started with a study of student progress, including high school courses completed, test scores, initial college choices, major changes, transfers, and completion

> **Practice**
> **Identify information sources**
>
> With the emphasis on accountability in educational systems and foundations supporting innovations, it is important for new and existing partnerships to develop strategies for collecting and using information for reporting to planning and budgeting groups that fund the interventions (e.g., boards, foundations, executive officers). Consider how information from data collection and analysis can inform your intervention strategies, but don't overlook the information routinely collected by the educational systems with which you work. Case 2.2 provides an example of a process of reviewing options for data collection.

within four years (see St. John & Musoba, 2010). The National Student Clearinghouse collects information on college students that can be accessed by high schools and state agencies for analyses of barriers to educational opportunities. In addition, colleges and universities collect data in their operating systems (e.g., admissions, registration) that can be used to identify barriers and evaluate the effects of interventions. But these data sources can be difficult for partnerships to attain, combine in appropriate ways, and analyze.

Surveys of participants in interventions provide an additional source of information that can be used in the evaluation process. However, since students often opt into interventions, it is difficult to control for this self-selection even when student tracking data are available; it is also difficult to select comparison students. Thus, the current standards for research are often difficult to meet. Nevertheless, it is important for partnerships to collect and use information related to their students when reporting to funding agencies.

Involving Researchers as Partners

University-based researchers (in the fields of education, economics, sociology, and public policy) may be interested in the issues being addressed by your partnership. When university researchers are involved, there is a higher probability that an evaluation study will contribute to the advancement of scholarship because of the incentives these researchers have to publish, which also means the study design will be rigorous in order to meet publishable standards. It is likely that if researchers are involved, they will need to obtain funding to pay for their staff, travel, and other expenses; your organization will benefit from these activities. But it is important to recognize that researchers and practitioners often talk in different languages, so communication must remain open.

Analyze changes using data and information from existing sources to identify possible interventions. Collaboration on assessing challenges requires considering alternative perspectives. Too frequently, practitioners, researchers, and policymakers think they already know the solution—and advocate for a specific program or remedy—before the process begins. Indeed, these predispositions provide the motivation to engage in planning groups. But members of these groups and the researchers with whom they work need to focus on identifying underlying causes of challenges before trying to solve them through quick policy solutions (i.e., pulling "policy levers") and new requirements for practitioners.

Working together, researchers and practitioners can identify alternative reasons for gaps in access and success that can be the focus of inquiry-based change. Some factors to consider include the following:

- *Compare key indicators of equity and achievement outcomes.* The public accountability systems used in K–12 and higher education usually include data on outcomes, but frequently further analysis is required to (a) identify gaps across racial and income groups and (b) explore the relationships among factors that relate to outcomes.
- *Identify possible barriers to academic success within and between partner schools and colleges.* Think together about the possible causes of underachievement and departure. The most critical challenges relate to groups that underachieve or are more likely to depart. If a system has much lower-than-average achievement and higher-than-usual departure, it is likely the system as a whole faces challenges.
- *Collect additional information from existing sources at partner organizations, such as reports from prior studies and focus group interviews.* There are often prior studies which should be reviewed to gain better understanding of social background, ethnicity, program implementation, impact of concerns about educational

costs, and other topics related to any problems uncovered. It is crucial to build informed, collective judgments from extant data to, if possible, identify strategies that can be pilot tested.

- *Collect additional data if needed to examine barriers for students and families that can be addressed through interventions by the partnership.* Existing research may or may not be sufficient to make informed judgments about critical challenges. Sometimes additional research is needed, but it takes time and funding.
- *Consider how possible interventions align with the challenges identified by the data analysis and reviews.* The partnership should have an *experimental attitude* focused on building shared understanding of how different types of interventions might work locally.
- *Develop and refine hypotheses.* Recognize there are limitations to hypothesized ideas of the underlying causes of problems; it is important to consider how these ideas might be tested. Ponder what might work and ways to test these hypotheses before making major investments or restructuring.
- *Avoid jumping directly to solutions.* Consider different strategies, including those currently being used and how successful strategies in one unit might be adapted by another.

Practice
Use existing information

While education reformers typically identify strategies that have worked elsewhere and try to replicate them, this overlooks the need for local solutions. Case 2.3 provides an example of using existing information to provide a baseline for planning for new student services. When possible, use existing information and resources to conduct analyses that do the following:

- Identify local challenges based on actual gaps in success
- Establish baseline outcomes to compare with outcomes after the intervention
- Consider successful local strategies that can be refined and adapted

Case 2.1
Projects Promoting Equity in Urban and Higher Education: Summit on Urban and Higher Education

Ed St. John

The summit, held in August 2009, was designed to create an opportunity for dialogue among a diverse participant group that included speakers and discussants representing reform initiatives in Washington, DC, and Detroit, Michigan; representatives of foundations engaged in outreach and other programs to promote access; University of Michigan (UM) faculty, staff, and graduate students engaged in outreach and student success projects; and representatives from Detroit schools. We started with an understanding of educational pathways and barriers (see Figure 1.1) and sought to learn from interventions that had worked in other locales.

At the time of the summit, Michigan was implementing new math requirements (i.e., Algebra II) for high school graduation. This strategy illustrates challenges inherent in the so-called education science approach to education reform, which emphasizes

- using data systems for control and regulation rather than for targeting reform at critical challenges;
- replicating practices thought to be best (e.g., new requirements) without adequately considering the challenges of implementation; and
- treating all students the same rather than designing interventions to meet local needs.

Challenges Facing Urban Schools

The summit focused on the critical challenges of urban education and diversity in higher education. In spite of more than two decades of reform efforts as part of the so-called excellence movement, high schools in most major cities did not have a successful history of graduating a majority of their students prepared for college. After a keynote by William Trent, the summit group discussed the role researchers have played in litigation promoting desegregation in education systems, as well as the increasing isolation of minorities in many urban school districts. At the time, it was evident that after the publication of *A Nation at Risk* (U.S. Department of Education, 1983) the percentage of students graduating from high school had declined and was an especially serious problem in urban schools. In addition, urban and suburban schools were more segregated than they were before *Brown v. Board of Education* in 1954. These compelling issues continue to merit serious attention. If American higher education is to achieve the dream of providing diverse learning communities that promote learning for all, a robust dialogue is crucial. There was a consensus that continued efforts to improve urban education were necessary for public universities to actualize their goal of graduating populations that represent the diversity of the residents of their states.

Learning From Successful Reforms

A focal point of the summit was learning the features of and research on two successful reform programs that had successfully raised rates of enrollment in two- and four-year colleges: (a) Twenty-First Century Scholars and related Indiana programs, presented by Scott Gillie, executive director of Encouragement Services, Inc.; and (b) Washington State Achievers (WSA), presented by Lorraine Solaegui, director of evaluation and research at College Success Foundation. While these two ongoing programs were different in design, they had the following common features:

- *Outreach and encouragement*: Both programs provided services to students as early as middle school, giving them access to information about college options and mentors.
- *Focus on improved preparation*: Both programs were aligned with initiatives to improve high school curriculum. Indiana introduced college preparatory curricula in all high schools and now has the Core 40 diploma[1] as the default option for graduation. WSA provided large grants to high schools to introduce advanced courses and form small schools within large high schools.
- *Student financial aid*: Both programs ensured students would have funding sufficient to pay for a four-year college. Twenty-First Century Scholars provided supplements to state grants to raise the total to equal public college tuition. WSA provided last-dollar grants topping off institutional and state grants within maximum award limits.

- *Support services for undergraduates*: WSA provided mentors during college, and Indiana was studying ways of improving support services during the college years.

Identifying New and Recurrent Barriers Facing Students

We started this venture by considering three challenges confronting students in Michigan as a consequence of the new high school graduation requirements (i.e., each student must complete a college preparatory course). The following three presentations sought to identify problems ahead:

1. *Math reform:* Nick Collins, director of the Center for Educational Outreach at UM, discussed UM's efforts to work with Martin Luther King Jr. High School in Detroit on math reform. *Challenge*: The teachers in Detroit schools required further preparation to teach advanced math courses to urban students.
2. *Literacy reform:* Lesley Rex, associate professor of education at UM, described a new method of intervening to improve critical literacy among high school students. *Challenge*: College preparation requires students to write at the collegiate level, a problem not addressed in the new state requirements.
3. *Social context:* Phillip Bowman, director of the National Center for Institutional Diversity and professor of higher education at UM, discussed the critical social issues facing urban high schools. *Challenge*: The social context of the lived lives of students must be considered for the new curriculum to successfully address the learning needs of Detroit students.

Contexts for Creating Urban Partnerships

The morning of the second day focused on learning about the following reform models underway in Washington, DC, and at UM:

- *Washington, DC*: John Williams, vice president for programs at Public Welfare Foundation, organized a consortium of researchers to develop projects supporting educational reform and outreach in Washington, DC. His work with researchers and policymakers

provided one emerging model for building research-school collaborations in urban settings.
- *UM*: In the aftermath of the passage of Proposal 2 in the state of Michigan—a voter initiative outlawing the use of affirmative action in college admissions—UM president Mary Sue Coleman established the Diversity Blueprints Commission to explore how the university would proceed into the future. A central recommendation of the commission was the establishment of a Center for Educational Outreach and Academic Success. Nick Collins summarized the Center's agenda. A capacity-building grant from the Ford Foundation focused on the support of the outreach and organizational change initiatives of the Center.

Reflective Questions

The Editors

1. How does the concentration of poverty and racial minorities in urban centers undermine efforts to promote equity in education?
2. How are the challenges to diversity at universities related to the difficult circumstances in urban schools?
3. How do the challenges in Detroit, Michigan; Washington, DC; and New Orleans, Louisiana, compare to the challenges your organization faces?

Case 2.2

College for Every Student: Assessment of Information Strategies

Rick Dalton and Ed St. John

College For Every Student (CFES) is a networking organization with more than two decades of experience organizing local school-college networks to provide social support for college access. Funded primarily by corporate foundations interested in improving the workforce, CFES has developed a distinctive approach to organizing within communities. Yet, like other networking organizations, it faces increasing pressures for reporting to funding agencies. We introduce the CFES organization and summarize results of the initial assessment of information needs.

Introducing CFES

Rick Dalton

CFES grew out of a three-year (spring 1983–spring 1986) study supported by the National Association for College Admission Counseling that identified best practices for raising students' college aspirations and increasing educational opportunities for underserved students through school-college partnerships (Holmes, 1986). Based on the results of a pilot program that boosted college-going 50% in 13 high schools in the southeast, CFES was founded in 1991 to develop and extend its unique partnership approach on a national scale. In the years that have followed, CFES has refined its approach with 700 K–12 public schools in rural and urban communities nationwide and significantly increased the graduation and college-going rates in participating schools. Between 2004 and 2008 over 3,000 students were encouraged by CFES to raise their academic performance and graduate from high school; 95% went on to college. By 2009, CFES was serving low-income students in 130 rural and urban schools with 210 college partners in 20 states and Washington, DC.

Among national organizations with similar college access missions, CFES has become an innovative school reform model in four respects. First, CFES enlists college students and graduates as mentors to engage K–12 students, most of whose parents did not attend college, in the preparation process. Second, CFES taps the potential of motivated high school students to serve as leaders and resources for effecting school change and helping other students learn the social skills to navigate the educational and social systems necessary for successful college transitions. Third, CFES is the only national nonprofit access program that specializes in turning around rural communities and schools by fostering family engagement in support of their children and building the cultural capital of the community. Fourth, the CFES model offers three core practices that work synergistically to encourage students to persist on a path toward college matriculation and graduation: mentors, pathways to college, and leadership through service. These features of the CFES model provide students, known as CFES scholars, with the skills to find a college that fits their interests and build the skills necessary for success in college.

By 2009, there were a growing number of college access organizations nationally. New state and federal programs required evaluations, and there was an increasing emphasis on research-based reform. Aware of these trends, the CFES Board of Directors requested a review of accountability systems used by the organization. All CFES students completed a brief questionnaire, and the schools provided annual plans and end-of-year summary reports, a system that has evolved over time. A summer intern with CFES reviewed research in the field and suggested a small number of researchers who might be able to provide guidance for the development of accountability and evaluation processes. As a step in strengthening the organization, I asked Ed St. John to visit and assess the prospects for a research partnership.

Review of Information, Data, and Evaluation Systems

Ed St. John

On October 7 and 8, 2009, I visited College For Every Student (CFES), a nonprofit organization in Cornwall, Vermont. I had the opportunity to review reporting systems, converse with staff on-site, and participate in a conference call with other staff and board members. This report summarizes: (a) understandings reached from my review of CFES reporting systems; (b) priorities for action with respect to reporting, evaluation, and research; and (c) possible next steps.

Summary of Report

The report focused on the data collected by CFES for assessment and evaluation. We used the following criteria:

- *Adequacy of internal accountability*: CFES had established forms that functioned relatively well in coordinating activities and reporting to the board. There is a functional system of internal accountability that program directors can buy into because it provides a

mechanism for securing support from CFES and donors. In addition, the reported graduation and college-going rates are important indicators of program success for donors and others.
- *Evaluation of and research on the impact of interventions*: These have become a high priority for public and private funding agencies, and evaluations for government agencies and foundations often require high methodological standards. While annual program reviews have been provided in the past, the higher standard of evaluation research has not been met. In addition, research that could support and inform organizational, programmatic, and professional development was not evident.
- *External reporting*: This involves providing evidence of program impact to current and potential funders, including government agencies. Ambiguity is evident relative to reporting to funding organizations based on accountability-oriented assessment. The need for impact evaluation has motivated a new generation of analyses using a more rigorous statistical standard, which is difficult for small programs to implement. Yet this type of evaluation is expected by those who want to consider the costs and benefits of interventions.

Analysis of Data Collection Options
The collection instruments are examined relative to the three criteria in Table 2.1. These instruments function as an internal monitoring system. From the data collected, it is apparent this process is functional for current operations. Based on conversations with staff in the office and during a subsequent conference call, there appears to be enthusiasm among program coordinators who derive personal benefits from engagement with students, staff, and teachers/faculty in partner schools and colleges.

While the current data collections serve the purpose of internal accountability, they do not meet contemporary statistical standards for independent evaluation that typically require a control group. Researchers perform random selection, and then selected and nonselected students are compared on critical outcomes. Randomized selection often poses problems in education and may even be of questionable value, depending on one's perspective. There are some statistical methods frequently used to

TABLE 2.1
CFES Reporting Instruments in Relation to Evaluation Criteria

Forms/criteria	Accountability	Evaluation	Reporting
CFES Aspiration Survey: Asks 12 yes-no questions	Serves as general indicator of student outcomes	This survey does not provide information for formative or summative evaluation of the program	To meet contemporary evaluation standards, it would be necessary to collect information from program and comparison students
CFES Plan: Lists planned activities related to core practices	Provides a basic form for internal accountability and control and a means of monitoring part-time personnel	Data sources are needed that lead to a classification of activities that could be examined in relation to school-level outcomes in the semiannual progress report	Not applicable
CFES Semiannual Progress Assessment: Provides a report on the progress of activities as well as data on 12th graders regarding CFES Scholars' graduation and college-going rates	Provides a detailed, activity-based mechanism for comparing plans for implementation; 12th-grade outcomes have been used for external reporting	Formative: The detailed information on activities can be examined (and classified) in relation to reported outcomes Summative: The self-reported information does not rise to current standards for evaluation	While the accountability-based model has worked for corporate funders to date, it could become problematic if and when a higher standard is required
Met Life Mentoring Survey: Asks 10 questions using Likert scale	New instrument with potential uses for formative evaluation and staff development for mentoring	Formative: This instrument could provide useful information to program coordinators and merits field-testing	Not applicable

integrate causal logic into the use of data on selected and nonselected students, including propensity score matching (PSM) and regression discontinuity (RD). Both of these methods would require using databases that were not available for the project.

To meet contemporary standards for obtaining new funding from major foundations or the U.S. Department of Education, new evaluations should be conducted. One intermediate possibility would be to alter the way data are collected from students, program coordinators, and schools to develop a set of indicators that would instill confidence in reviewers. Following are examples of current problems and possible solutions:

- *Uncertainty about the number of graduates and current students.* The semiannual survey asks about the number of CFES seniors, as well as how many of them graduated and how many went on to college. There are some problems with this type of data, including attrition from the student cohort since they enter the program early, usually in 9th or 10th grade. This is the same problem confronting other school districts that report graduation rates. In addition, the information on college-going is self-reported by the school, a form of data that generally is not used in evaluations. The federal government and state are currently spending millions of dollars to set up a system to track K–12 students across schools, which is well beyond the capacity of CFES. An alternative might be to collect data on graduates from the National Student Clearinghouse (NSC).
- *Ambiguity about efficacy of programs.* Good summative evaluation research is informed by theories of action (grounded ideas about how interventions actually link to outcomes; refer back to Figure 1.1). For example, the research conducted for the Gates Foundation on the Gates Millennial Scholars (GMS) program included surveys of students' experiences in college, a type of evaluation that has resulted in thoughtful research papers that have advanced the field of higher education and been useful in making program refinements.

Research that is informative relative to program effects should also be used in organizational and professional development, and it is important to ensure accuracy of cohort numbers (i.e., from 9th or 10th grade forward).

Reducing Uncertainty About Numbers
The most problematic issue was the uncertainty about numbers of students across years in the program. We discussed the following options:

- *Adding questions about the attrition (and potential addition) of students to cohorts as part of the semiannual report.* This would provide additional information on annual progress and program effects. While this would still be self-reported, it would yield more realistic numbers related to cohort graduation rates. The number of graduates who go on to college may be accurate (and they do vary across schools), but the uncertainty about the numbers and rates causes hesitation with respect to prima facie validity of the numbers.
- *Altering the forms for collecting data from program directors to include data on the number of contacts.* The current planning and progress forms provide a mechanism for communication about activities; however, since there is no codification of activities (counts in relation to type), these data are not routinely summarized. One possibility would be to codify the activities included in plans and alter the semiannual report into a form that can be more easily understood.
- *Collecting data on college-going for graduating seniors (CFES Scholars and others) at a sample of high schools.* These data could be used to assess program effects, provided an appropriate matching procedure could be developed.

Improving information to inform program effectiveness and development represents another possible priority. Some possible studies discussed included the following:

- *Survey of students.* The mentoring, leadership through service, and pathways to college CFES core practices relate directly to the core constructs of social capital (as proposed by Coleman [1988] and developed through sociology research)—mentors, networks, and information—as functional forms of capital that can improve academic success. The researcher in me thought it would be interesting to study these links, and I have doctoral students who could do so. There are some issues related to human subjects, student

response timing, and data collection procedures that would need to be addressed in order to achieve this aim.
- *Site visits to schools.* In collaboration with graduate students, I am currently conducting a study of high schools across the United States. It may be possible to combine my interest in the study of high schools with Dalton's apparent interest in the ethnographic study of students. We could conduct interviews with teachers and school officials along with focus group interviews with students to generate useful information for the program and provide a data source for additional research.
- *Survey of program directors.* We discussed the idea of conducting a survey of program coordinators focused on their professional development, a step that could inform organizational development in CEFS and be of research value.

Reconciling Aims and Setting Priorities
Practicality is important relative to the goals of reducing ambiguity in numbers and improving information on effectiveness. Putting these two sets of issues together, priorities could include the following:

- Developing a student questionnaire that can be completed online, focusing on specific activities and students' engagement in them. This approach might meet both goals, but it would need to be carefully planned. Ideally, this could be pilot tested and brought to scale as a new organizational capacity for data collection.
- Investigating the option of collecting data for graduating classes of seniors from a select group of high schools. Propensity score matching on student background variables could be used to find a group to compare to students in CFES.
- Collaborating on a study of high schools—and maybe middle schools—as a means of building an understanding of program effects. This could include interviews with students, teachers, and program coordinators.
- Developing and pilot testing a new reporting system for program coordinators and schools, possibly inclusive of engagement and background information that would be informative for purposes of research evaluation.

> **Reflective Questions**
>
> The Editors
>
> 1. How does the mission of CFES relate to the challenges discussed at the summit on urban schools?
> 2. How has the emphasis on public accountability and causal research methods influenced the conversation about the uses of data to inform change to improve educational pathways?
> 3. How do the CFES core practices—pathways, mentoring, and leadership through service—relate to the general theory of change?
> 4. If you were on the CFES board, what more would you like to know about the organization and related outcomes? Would the recommended solutions address the challenges posed by the board?

Case 2.3

Baseline Assessment: Student Achievement in Detroit's New, Old, and Closed Public High Schools

Ed St. John

Our capacity-building efforts in Detroit through the DPS–Higher Education Consortium used research to support targeted reforms to address critical challenges, emphasizing

- analyses of longitudinal databases and locally situated qualitative studies to examine underlying reasons for critical challenges;
- support for collaborative planning involving university researchers, high school educators, parents, and other community members in the design and testing of targeted interventions;
- interventions focused on reducing inequality in educational opportunity and improving opportunities for underrepresented students, raising their quality of education to equal that of majority students; and
- evaluations of whether interventions actually improve achievement and reduce inequality.

To illustrate the way public data can be used in assessment, we used publicly available data to examine student achievement in Detroit public schools. More than most urban school districts, Detroit engaged in closing public schools and opening new charters in the early 2000s. The closures of schools may have been necessary because of population decline coupled with decline in per-student funding by the state. When students leave public schools to attend charter schools, their per-student funding follows them to their new schools, further decreasing the capacity of urban school districts to keep local schools open. After summarizing patterns of achievement in new, old, and closed high schools, we raise a few questions for readers.

Achievement in New and Old High Schools

The ACT college admissions exam was used for 11th graders in Michigan in 2007 and 2010. The comparison of scores by school type reveals mostly minor differences in scores. Four DPS high schools were closed between 2007 and 2010 so we could compare their scholars with those in newly opened schools after 2000. The average ACT scores in 2007 for the four closed high schools were slightly higher than the newly opened schools, but lower than the high schools that stayed open. Further, the new and old charter high schools had slightly lower ACT scores than the continuing public schools in 2007.

There was slight improvement in the ACT scores for charter high schools between 2007 and 2010 (Table 2.2). Yet in 2010 the average ACT score in continuing public high schools was modestly higher than in the newly opened charters and modestly lower than in the older charter schools. The 2010 ACT scores differed by more than a standard deviation in only one cross-group comparison: The average ACT score in newly opened public high schools (14.08) was more than a standard deviation lower than the average score in the older charter high schools (15.56). All groups of high schools had ACT scores below the national average, but comparisons to the national average on the ACT are somewhat problematic because only a few states use the ACT as a statewide exam for 11th graders. Given the range of average ACT scores across high school types in 2010 (14.08 to 15.56), all types of Detroit high schools faced challenges with respect to improvement in academic preparation for college.

TABLE 2.2
Average ACT Composite Score for the 11th Grade by School Type: 2007 and 2010

	2007		2010	
School Type	N	Mean	N	Mean
DPS newly open during 2000–2010	2	14.40	5	14.08
		(1.13)		(1.30)
DPS closed during 2000–2010	4*	14.43	-	-
		(0.22)		-
DPS stayed open during 2000–2010	26	15.12	25	15.00
		(1.96)		(1.98)
Charter newly open during 2000–2010	12	14.43	12	14.89
		(1.06)		(1.32)
Charter stayed open during 2000–2010	7	14.59	7	15.56
		(0.72)		(1.08)

Source. Michigan Department of Education.
Note. Standard deviations in parentheses.
*Four DPS high schools were closed between 2007 and 2010—Mackenzie, Northern, Murray-Wright, and Redford.

The theory of school choice has long assumed that more choice is better for students, but the research has not confirmed the benefits. But these analyses, consistent with national research (e.g., Ravitch, 2010), find that charter schools did not have higher achievement than Detroit public high schools. Students who change schools during high school are potentially at greater risk than students who have stable learning environments. The analysis of elementary and middle schools revealed similar findings about student achievement. Students who face severe challenges because of declining social structures and increasing poverty are at higher risk in situations that require them to transfer because their schools have closed.

> **Reflective Questions**
>
> The Editors
>
> This analysis was part of studies prepared for the Detroit Schools–Higher Education Consortium (DS-HEC) during the start-up process (see Case 2.3). This group included representatives from Detroit schools and colleges in the area.
>
> 1. What does this slice of information on achievement indicate about the advantages and disadvantages of new schools versus continuing old schools?
> 2. What might be common challenges in public and charter high schools? What different challenges might they face?
> 3. What additional information would help inform your understanding of the educational challenges facing urban high school students?
> 4. In 2011 all students were required to complete Algebra II for graduation. Do you expect this change will increase ACT scores and/or student dropout rates?
> 5. What factors should DS-HEC examine to evaluate the impact of the new graduation requirements?
> 6. How might local colleges work with high schools to improve student achievement and implementation of new graduation requirements?

Note

1. The Core 40 requires advanced courses in math, science, language, and other fields thought to be necessary for admission to a four-year college.

3

ORGANIZING FOR CHANGE

> **Guidance 3: Organizing for Change**
>
> 1. *Recognize strengths of partners*: Researchers, advocates, and practitioners have knowledge, skills, and commitments that can inform and support reform initiatives. Organizing for change builds on the strengths of the different partners. The cases in this chapter provide examples of organizing for engaged scholarship promoting educational reform.
> 2. *Undertake feasible initiatives*: Partners frequently can try out new approaches with existing resources, and information from trials can inform future reforms. The cases illustrate potential organizing strategies in community-based organizations, schools, and state systems.
> 3. *Use action inquiry*: Information generation from engaged scholarship provides resources that change advocates can use to create opportunities, change practices, and transform organizations as illustrated by the educational cases.

Organizing is a core process in reforms that seek to expand student learning opportunities, especially in collaborations among schools, colleges, communities, and researchers. Unfortunately, the systemic approaches typically used in organizational reform are not well aligned with the research process. Educators pursue their own aims while complying with organizational requirements, while researchers typically conceive of research in a pseudoscience frame. Often the result is research critical of policy and practice, along with prescriptive change models that are adopted, adapted, or rejected by educators.

This chapter encourages organizing to use information to promote equity within schools and colleges and in networks that support students. The guide for action focuses on building workable partnerships, using research to support organizational changes and adaptations that promote equity by improving college opportunities, and communication among partners. It also provides a framework for researchers to bring into their scholarship. The case studies examine

- development of a research strategy using tracking data for students graduating from high school in Washington, DC (Case 3.1);
- the iterative process of organizing in partnership with CFES (Case 3.2); and
- organizing in Detroit, Michigan (Case 3.3).

To maximize the value of the guidance in this chapter, we encourage readers to quickly review the three cases as a means of learning how to develop their own strategies for change promoting equity.

Guide for Action

Organizing partnerships among social justice advocates and researchers interested in promoting equity provides a mechanism for promoting interventions to remedy barriers to student opportunity. These partnerships take many forms; to have a role in the improvement process, they must be aligned with formal organizational governing mechanisms. Partnerships promoting social justice should use evidence about inequalities and prospective remedies to inform advocacy for adaptive changes that rebalance equity issues with the efficiency and accountability narratives that dominate educational organizations. Whether new partnerships become sustainable or remain informal depends on funding, organizational commitment, and other factors. To inform the organizing process, we focus on the following four key tasks:

1. *Reduce inequality* by developing new initiatives and organizing work groups to develop and test intervention strategies.

2. *Identify feasible projects.* Both social justice advocates and researchers benefit from quick turnaround projects that do not require additional funding and help them learn about strategies for change.
3. *Include evaluation in the design of interventions.* Evaluation of outcomes is necessary in reports to participants and funding organizations. It is easier to provide the kind of data needed if evaluation is considered in advance.
4. *Coordinate the research process*—conducting, vetting, reviewing, and disseminating findings—with the interests of funding agencies, including planning and budgeting in partner organizations.

Focus on Reducing Inequality

The current educational system has been on a trajectory toward greater inequality over the past three decades, as an artifact of economic and policy changes. Once inequalities in the current system have been identified, it is possible to organize strategies for change. Practices that facilitate rapid change include the following:

- *Link research projects with strategies used by change-oriented organizations*: Find organizations that share your goals and design projects that will provide the data you need to move forward.
- *Use action projects to build shared understanding*: In the three cases in this chapter, specific projects emerged based on the interests and needs of partner organizations. The results were discussed within the partnership so a mutual understanding of outcomes could be determined; results were also reported to others as needed.
- *Align research with advocacy and governance*: Results from research projects can be used to inform advocates and policy decisions.

It is important for readers to consider how to align people around critical challenges as they form partnerships and build organizational capacity. Sometimes affiliations are temporary, as in the Indiana Project on Academic Success (IPAS), but some evolve beyond the project. In both the CFES and the Detroit Consortium cases there was evidence of capacity building.

Identify Feasible Projects

Partnerships, networks, or consortia of institutions take form as members begin to understand the types of information needed to address shared critical challenges. In IPAS we organized state-wide and regional initiatives for working college students along with innovations in instruction supporting diversity, community college transfer, and other topics. The development of a regional work group in Gary, Indiana, was particularly productive (Moore & Rago, 2009; Ziskin, Torres, Hossler, & Gross, 2010), resulting in a book that developed new logics for supporting working students (Perna, 2012). With this success in mind, along with the national visibility of the Consortium on Chicago School Research at the University of Chicago (ccsr.uchicago.edu), we were motivated to encourage organizing efforts in Washington, DC (DC), and Detroit, Michigan, (Detroit) with mixed success. The Detroit and DC cases merit study by social justice advocates seeking to build new coalitions.

- *Align partnerships.* In all three of this chapter's cases (DC, CFES, and Detroit), organizational partners identified researchers to conduct the studies that supported organizational changes to improve student outcomes (as we discuss in Chapter 4). The urgency of having usable information proved to be the major factor informing the projects chosen.
- *Identify organizing strategies.* Actionable projects that promote social justice have value for students, practitioners engaged in the process, and researchers who stretch beyond the boundaries of traditional theoretical frameworks to address problems in practice. Researchers must conduct studies with sound, dependable methods. Partner organizations' theories of change must inform the research design and data collection.

Evaluation May Come First

We consistently find that practitioners understand the value of research when the inquiry process starts with an evaluation of current practice. Practitioners are often anxious for information when they first engage in partnerships. Based on experience working with numerous groups, we conceptualized the inquiry process with the possibility of starting with preliminary evaluation research (see Figure 3.1). When these initial studies focus on what is being done well and what could be done better, the results can be used to jump-start inquiry into ways of improving outcomes.

Figure 3.1. Role of preliminary evaluation in the action inquiry cycle: The short loop through inquiry.

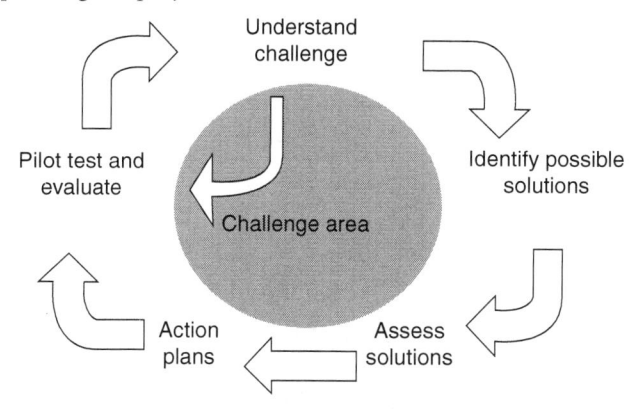

Challenge area
- Understand challenge
- Identify possible solutions
- Assess solutions
- Action plans
- Pilot test and evaluate

Practice
Start with feasible projects to inform practice

Educators are often wary of research because of the burdensome nature of public accountability systems, while researchers are often steeped in tautological theories that are essentially true but useless in promoting change. To begin the shift from replicating inequality to changing the ways systems work, choose a project that is feasible and will inform the partnership. In your review of the organizing cases in this chapter consider the following:

- How did the researchers and organizers discover topics that were useful to both partners?
- How well did the projects align with critical needs raised by partner organizations?
- What issues remained unaddressed and why? Consider organizational factors, data limitations, and researcher biases.
- How can your partnership move quickly to evaluation and research topics that inform advocacy for underrepresented students?

Include Evaluation in the Design of Interventions

It is increasingly necessary to include evaluation as part of reform projects initiated by foundations and large educational systems (e.g., school districts and universities). As much as possible, evaluation efforts should not only follow sound practices for external reporting but also provide information in a form working groups can use. When researchers work in collaboration with reform-oriented work groups, it is possible to generate not only information that guides reform but also, if the action researchers are interested, publications that inform the education improvement process. The entire group should be involved in starting up new initiatives through action inquiry. Related practices include the following:

- *Developing databases* for use in the support of planning, reporting, and budgeting by the steering group, creating transparent information on progress
- *Working with databases* to conduct studies of interest on their campuses
- *Developing student surveys and/or conducting focus groups* to collect information on student experiences, providing feedback and analysis to inform ongoing operations
- *Collaborating with members of work groups* in schools, colleges, community organizations, and academic departments, providing reviews and analyses that support and inform partners
- *Participating in and contributing to the research-based dialogue* about strategies for improving academic success

Action researchers should be encouraged to participate in workshops and research conferences and, as appropriate, write or colloborate on academic papers on their research. If the action inquiry approach is new to the organization, institutional researchers in particular need exposure to the process; if an external researcher is brought in, the relationship with institutional research needs to be negotiated with care.

Coordinate the Research Process

The roles of the organization and the researcher should be clearly defined, along with time frames and products. Researchers need the academic freedom to reach their own findings, partner organizations must have the opportunity to vet the work, and publications should protect human subjects. Following the rules of research protects researchers, the organizations with which they work, and participants. In partnerships promoting social justice, researchers involved in engaged scholarship research can complete high-quality scholarship that meets generally accepted standards, which makes it more likely that they will be able to publish their work and contribute to the work of partner organizations. Scholarship that falls short of this standard can actually harm partner organizations; qualitative research that excludes critical findings can end up reinforcing exclusionary practices, and quantitative research that overlooks the relationship between interventions and outcomes can be used to rationalize unproven reforms as though they are research-based. Using an actionable theory of change (chapter 1) helps researchers think through these problems.

Most large projects require or at least encourage some form of evaluation. If the projects routinely undertaken in an organization align with the interests of graduate students and other researchers, it is often possible for them to perform the evaluation as part of an engaged research project. We encourage readers to reflect on the challenges of forming workable research partnerships. None of the cases we present are perfect. All have strengths and weaknesses, but all involve researchers and practitioners working in partnership. We recommend voluntary, rather than required, engagement in research partnerships in both the organizational and academic settings.

Vetting and Releasing Research

Another issue is how to release findings. Local news media like to report critical challenges facing schools as well as successful interventions. The problem with "going public" comes when findings do not support the organization's agenda. We recommend leaving publicity to the practitioners and their organizations and scholarship to the researchers. As long as academic publications comply with research standards, data agreements, and protection of human subjects, there should not be a problem with valuing the researchers' interest in making academic contributions.

Finding System Support for Change

Using action inquiry—especially building research-based evidence—provides work groups with means of increasing awareness of challenges and opportunities for change within educational systems. Ideally, research evidence can be used when requesting and obtaining funding, either new funding or redefining work agendas within organizations. Funding agencies and the nonprofit organizations they fund have an interest in the continuing success of endeavors. Funding agencies often adapt the rationales used in education governance, including the logics of efficiency, accountability, and market incentives.

By building research evidence, change advocates bring new substance to the organizational change process, potentially breaking through the status-maintaining aspect of actions by vested interest groups. Educational systems have formal procedures for distributing and redistributing funding, but they often reinforce vested interests that perpetuate class reproduction through inequality in educational opportunities. The social justice aspect of action inquiry—explicit in its emphasis on addressing critical social challenges that emerge within educational systems—provides a rationale for targeted projects that address critical challenges, including alterations in funds distribution (i.e., criteria or indicators used to rationalize funding decisions). In market-oriented funding models, dollars follow students. Accordingly, expanding opportunity and retaining students translate directly into dollar flow into the organization, which means it is important to use research evidence to redirect funding toward improving enrollment. Traditional budgeting models use formal rationales, including research-based evidence, as part of budget allocations. In either case, it is crucial to bring an awareness of funding mechanisms into the process.

A Bottom-Up Vantage

Using action inquiry to build partnerships provides a mechanism for involving community groups, students, and educators in the change process to accomplish goals like realigning student support and other services that promote engaged learning. Partnerships can change the rhetorical blame game into an evidence-based change process, focusing on creating new remedies to recurrent or emergent challenges to fairness and equity.

Continually think about opportunities to involve partners in finding solutions and include and respect the voices of individuals and groups normally left outside of the system. Bringing diverse voices into deliberations on policy and practice is vital to actualizing a renewed emphasis on social justice in education. It is difficult to get representation of all stakeholders, but it is important to make sure those who are usually left out are included in the working group. It is also crucial that one person or a few people in powerful positions do not become the loudest voices at the table.

Case 3.1
Washington, DC: Organizing a Local Network

Ed St. John and Rehva Jones McKinnon

In Projects Promoting Equity in Urban and Higher Education we sought to develop research partnerships that promoted equity through improved preparation, pathways to college, and support of college completion for underrepresented students. The initial organizing effort was in Washington, DC (DC), a city in the midst of change. This case describes the organizing process, along with efforts in the DC Office of the State Superintendent of Education (OSSE) to use the capacities provided by research partners. Readers are encouraged to reflect on how both practitioners and researchers can shape the formation of research partnerships.

The DC Consortium Start-Up

Ed St. John

The DC Research Consortium on College Access and Retention was organized by John B. Williams in 2009. It consisted of individual researchers and educators who aspired to produce, disseminate, and utilize research on college access and retention involving DC public school students. Participants were drawn from a variety of institutions and voluntarily associated themselves with the consortium.

Developing a Mission
The consortium developed a mission focusing on producing research and other systematic inquiry useful for solving problems and gaining insights to increase the number of DC students who finish high school and enroll in and graduate from college. The school-to-college graduation pipeline was the primary concern of consortium participants. They focused on the city's expanding and diversifying K–12 system as well as the local colleges and universities the system's graduates would attend. Individuals

contributing to the consortium's work included university faculty and administrators, policy researchers, foundation officials, government officials, and independent consultants. The consortium adopted the following principles of operation:

- The research conducted must be of very high quality.
- Researchers who conduct inquiry projects, educators, and those who might use the research findings should be involved in all stages.
- Findings from the research should be widely disseminated and made available to anyone who plans to put them to good use.
- Membership in the consortium consists of individuals who hold expertise useful for accomplishing its mission.
- The work should complement and coordinate with similar efforts by other organizations, since the need is substantial and opportunities for making a contribution should not be competitively driven.

The consortium met on a monthly basis during the spring of 2009 to establish its membership, develop internal operations, assess support for the consortium's research mission, discuss important research topics, and establish a research agenda. While the planning effort was funded by a Ford Foundation planning grant, the Ford Foundation ultimately decided against proceeding with the DC project. Ultimately, we were unable to identify potential funding sources but made progress on a research agenda and development of a database.

Establishing a Research Agenda
Planning started with identifying and assessing current and emerging data sources that could be used for research on college access and retention for DC students. We contacted other groups interested in these issues, including the DC Consortium of Universities, the Double the Numbers steering committee, the DC Office of the State Superintendent, the DC Public Schools, and the University of the District of Columbia (UDC).

We were particularly pleased to receive the cooperation of the DC OSSE. The collaboration with OSSE focused on the need for research and inquiry to improve and expand the DC college pipeline. Most participants agreed that systematically collected information and research findings, reported on a regular and continuing basis, would be very helpful. Meetings of consortium participants and discussions with potential partners were promising. We encountered the encouraging but frustrating problem of responding quickly to a wide variety of requests for information.

Dawn Williams, a professor from Howard University, was commissioned to prepare a background paper reviewing prior research on college access and retention of DC students. We investigated federal and local data sources for conducting research on the student pipeline. Initially, the following four areas of research were explored based upon the interests and expertise of consortium participants and recommendations gathered from discussions with important stakeholders in the pipeline:

1. Assessment of the pipeline over time was considered, with a history as a topic that had been raised in a DC Double the Numbers Report that recommended undertaking comprehensive studies of the pipeline on a regular basis to help double the numbers of students completing college in the district because aspects of the college pipeline were constantly changing. We sought to develop a database that would support this type of research.
2. The district's student financial aid programs emerged as critical because of congressional questions about tuition assistance grants (the District of Columbia Tuition Assistance Grant [DC TAG]).
3. The participation of UDC was of interest, providing an appropriate database could be developed. UDC had a high dropout rate and, as a consequence, there was interest in developing of a community college focused on enabling more DC students to complete the first two years of college.
4. There was a shared interest in high-quality scholarship on the district's rich and diverse college access advocacy community. Research on these organizations could describe how they are designed to provide and facilitate access and graduation from college, problems they are encountering, and proposals for assisting them.

Leaders and officials expressed the need for constructive research in all these areas and promised cooperation with the consortium's efforts. Tentatively, the consortium would concentrate on designing specific research projects that appropriately described, analyzed, and reported on the district's student aid program, the role of UDC, and the contributions of the college access community.

Once we established an explicit focus on the DC TAG program, it was possible to develop an agreement to generate data from existing data systems and from a request to the National Student Clearinghouse to track students through college.

OSSE's Involvement in the DC Research Consortium

Rehva Jones McKinnon

Prior to the 2000–2001 school year, DC students who pursued higher education had only one affordable public choice: UDC. Employing a "one-size-fits-all" strategy, UDC had an open-admissions policy; students seeking admissions to more selective public institutions were forced to leave the district and pay out-of-state tuition. During this time, roughly 64% of the district's college-bound residents enrolled at institutions outside of the district; nationally, only 15% of students attended colleges outside their state (Kane, 2004, p. 1). Slightly more than two-thirds of the DC students attending schools outside the district went to private institutions, which was double the national rate. As a result, traditional-age college students from DC paid twice the national average for annual tuition despite the fact that the district had one of the highest poverty rates in the nation, 16.5% (Lazere, 2007, p. 1).

Bipartisan district and congressional officials, concerned business executives, community leaders, and citizens crafted a solution to the district's dilemma. Championed by Congresswoman Eleanor Holmes Norton, then president Bill Clinton signed the District of Columbia's College Access Act, Public Law 106-98, on November 12, 1999. This legislation moved through both the House and the Senate with amazing speed after being introduced in March 1999. The legislation created two programs: (a) the District of Columbia College Access Program (DCCAP) to provide college guidance and counseling to public high school students and (b) the DC TAG program to significantly reduce the cost of college for district residents by bridging the gap between in-state and out-of-state tuition. Since its inception, DC TAG has enjoyed the full support of both Democrat and Republican presidents. Under President George W. Bush, the program was reauthorized in 2007, and its appropriation doubled from $17 million to $35.1 million. DC TAG provides grants of up to $10,000 per academic year for up to five years for attendance at public four-year colleges and universities throughout the United States, Guam, the U.S. Virgin Islands, and Puerto Rico. The grant also provides up to $2,500 per academic year for up to five years toward tuition at private colleges in the Washington, DC, metropolitan area; private historically Black colleges and universities (HBCUs); and two-year colleges nationwide.

Prior to funding reauthorizations, DC TAG was not need- or merit-based. The 2007 reauthorization affixed an upper limit of $1 million per family in taxable income. DC TAG grantees attend elite public institutions, such as the University of Maryland, University of Virginia, University of Michigan, Pennsylvania State University, and the University of California; HBCUs with legacies of excellence, such as Morehouse and Spelman; and local institutions, such as Trinity Washington, Georgetown, Howard, Catholic, George Washington, and American University (Jones, 2004, p. 4).

Opportunity for Partnership With the DC Research Consortium
In June 2007, DC's Public Education Reform Amendment Act (PERAA) was passed into law (District Law 17-9). This legislation brought significant changes to the district's public education landscape, including

- establishing DC Public Schools as a cabinet-level agency under the authority of the mayor;
- creating the role of chancellor of public schools;
- establishing a Department of Education headed by a deputy mayor for education; and
- amending the State Education Office Establishment Act of 2000 to change the name to the Office of the State Superintendent of Education (OSSE), transferring and assigning state-level education agency functions to this expanded agency.

PERAA called for the OSSE to design and execute a public merger and acquisition that consolidated education functions previously residing within four District of Columbia government agencies with 800 government employees. In 2009, still experiencing merger and acquisition aftershocks, the OSSE suffered from additional inertia brought about by an abrupt change in executive leadership. The agency was working through new and ever-evolving internal structures, politics, policies, and processes. The DC Research Consortium's proposal represented the first time the new agency was approached to participate in a research effort.

The DC TAG program was one of the more mature programs within the newly established state education agency. The program was well-funded administratively and programmatically with leadership that had emerged from within its rank and file. A five-year plan focused on building strong systems for capturing and reporting accurate data was being diligently implemented. OSSE was well positioned to fulfill legislative reporting requirements because of the establishment of new application policies, most notably the required completion of the Free Application for Federal Student Aid (FAFSA); membership in the National Student Clearinghouse; and the DC OneApp, the program's application database launched in 2006 after the successful migration of several legacy data systems. Moreover, these accomplishments enabled the program to fully leverage the DC Research Consortium's proposal. The timing of the partnership was serendipitous as the 2009–2010 school year marked the 10-year anniversary of the DC TAG program as well as its reauthorization. The work products resulting from the research partnership would include comprehensive reports, marketing materials to raise awareness of the DC TAG program, and a report on the postsecondary progress of its grantees; these products would establish the OSSE as the "go-to" source for accurate and reliable data on postsecondary preparation, pursuit, and persistence for DC residents.

Reflective Questions

The Editors

1. How did the interests of researchers and local educational organizations influence the formation of the consortium?
2. What influenced the OSSE decision to join in the partnership by requesting a specific study?
3. How might organizers of the DC Consortium move forward with the venture after the Ford Foundation decided not to continue the project?

Case 3.2

CFES: Organizing the Research Partnership

Rick Dalton and Ed St. John

The strategies used to organize a research partnership between CFES and the University of Michigan (UM) Team are summarized.

1. Dalton discusses the refined alignment of core practices and annual organizing strategy.
2. St. John summarizes efforts to build a reporting system and evaluation capacity.

Using Research to Inform Strategic Initiatives

Rick Dalton

While CFES had information that could support the organization internally, it had not focused on developing a research-based approach that could be communicated externally, a strategy that emerged through the collaboration with the UM Team. CFES made significant changes between 2009 and 2013, informed in part by research projects with the UM Team. CFES has refined its core practices to focus explicitly on academic capital formation (social, cultural, and human capital focused on uplift) among underrepresented students and aligned its research partnership with its semiannual program directors' retreats.

Core Practices Facilitate Academic Capital Formation (ACF)
As part of their engagement in CFES, schools develop their own procedures for selecting students as CFES Scholars. Although CFES asks schools to target low-income students (as determined by free or reduced lunch), the ultimate selection of the CFES Scholar cohort is left to the school. In some cases, schools target underresourced cohorts, such as students with GPAs between 2.5 and 3.5, or high-risk groups, such as young men of color. In other cases, schools require students to apply to participate and selection is based on the student's desire to be part of CFES.

Core Practices

Schools in urban and rural areas have established a college culture through intensive exposure to higher education, mentoring, and leadership through service practices. The goal in all CFES schools is to help low-income, first-generation students prepare for, gain access to, and successfully transition to college. This goal aligns with the theory of academic capital formation. Components of the CFES strategy include the following:

- Enabling college students, community leaders, teachers, and peers to work with K–12 students in a process that engages them in college readiness
- Tapping the potential of K–12 students to serve as leaders who effect school change and help peers learn how to navigate educational and social systems in order to make successful transitions to college. As part of the annual organizing process in schools, CFES Scholars plan and execute activities that help make "their schools and communities better places"
- Using three core practices—mentoring, pathways to college, and leadership through service—to encourage students to pursue a path toward college. These features of the CFES model provide students, known as CFES Scholars, with the skills to find colleges that fit their interests and build the skills necessary for success in college.

  1. *Mentoring:* Relationships between CFES Scholars and college students, teachers, community members, other adults, and peers foster personal and academic growth. Mentors are student advocates, encouraging college preparation activities, fostering value clarification, providing career and college orientation, and building study skills that raise CFES Scholars' sense of what is possible.
  2. *Pathways to college:* College partnerships allow CFES Scholars to visit college campuses, interact with college students and faculty, and gain exposure to admissions, financial aid, and academic program faculty. Additional exposure to college opportunities occurs through workshops for parents and CFES Scholars on how to choose a college and complete college admissions and financial aid applications, as well as summer on-campus programs to raise college aspirations and convince lower-income parents that financial obstacles are surmountable.

3. *Leadership through service*: This component of the CFES reform model builds student leadership skills through school and service opportunities that empower young people to take responsibility for others and build self-esteem, resilience, discipline, and organizational skills.

Organizational Strategies
The following is a brief overview of CFES's annual organizing process that creates a culture of change:

- *Semiannual program director retreats.* Two-day retreats in August and February provide program directors from across the globe an opportunity to plan, refine strategies, and learn from one another.
- *Regional planning and training workshop.* In the late summer, each school sends members of its CFES team to a regional planning and training workshop. The program focuses on developing a year-long plan to integrate the three core practices. Participants receive support from CFES professional staff in team building, strengthening college partnerships, and moving students toward college readiness through CFES practices.
- *Ongoing support from CFES program directors.* CFES program directors provide professional support to help school teams meet their objectives. They regularly visit the schools and meet with educators and Scholars; they provide college knowledge, leadership development, and other support directly to Scholars.
- *CFES National Conference.* Each November, CFES team members join colleagues from other CFES schools from the United States and Ireland at the annual CFES National Conference. The National Conference includes speakers and workshops on cutting-edge strategies that promote college access for low-income students.
- *Professional development for CFES teams.* Each month, CFES staff lead professional development sessions on-site for educators and students.
- *Training and programming for CFES Scholars.* Scholars participate in CFES-facilitated activities throughout the year designed to support college access and success. Programs include peer mentoring

training, leadership development workshops, best practices expos, student leadership summits, and virtual (online) trainings.
- *College Explore.* A program that provides rising juniors and seniors opportunities to spend a weekend on higher education campuses during the summer.

Culture Supporting Uplift

CFES serves about 60,000 students annually across the United States. CFES works with both rural and urban schools that serve a range of ages and levels of ability and preparation. Educators and Scholars embrace the CFES approach because of its simplicity and power. Every component feeds into the same goal: ensuring that students are college-ready. In the United States, educators have grown weary of programs and strategies that exist one year but are gone the next. The CFES core practices produce long-term results. Research evidence shows that, through building academic, social, and cultural capital, the practices improve achievement, build leadership capacity, promote civic engagement, and ultimately ensure that students graduate from high school ready for college.

Students are both recipients and drivers of the CFES program, and they relish their identity as CFES Scholars. They participate through in-person and virtual programs that take place both on-site at their schools and on college campuses. Through Skype, FaceTime, and other platforms, CFES Scholars can also participate in leadership summits and peer mentor trainings with peers across the globe.

Integrating Research Into CFES Annual Organizing

Ed St. John

The process of developing a research orientation within CFES took trial and error, as is the case in many learning situations. I briefly summarize an evaluation plan we developed and tried out in efforts to take CFES interventions to scale and a qualitative study of four rural schools, as an illustration of our school-based work.

Alignment With Education Research Standards
With the encouragement of a CFES board member, Rick Dalton and I worked with an experienced proposal writer to consider research strategies that could be systematic and provide information aligned with the type and quality of research necessary to bring innovations to scale. We both learned from the process. Following are some of the options we explored:

- *National data:* CFES considered developing and implementing an online student tracking and reporting system that used college enrollment data derived from the National Student Clearinghouse on CFES Scholars who graduated from high school. We found this would not be feasible in the schools CFES worked with, partly because it was too expensive.
- *Internal tracking:* CFES explored the possibility of using a web-based system developed by Encouragement Systems, Inc. (ESI), for tracking students through annual survey data on students' background, aspirations (educational and career), and other interests. ESI presented twice at the CFES annual conference, and one school pilot tested the system. This pilot test revealed the following problems:
  - *Limited computer access:* Only a small percentage of CFES schools had routine access to computers.
  - *Questions not well aligned with CFES practices:* While the ESI survey had questions related to common practices in Gaining Early Awareness and Readiness for Undergraduate Programs (GEAR UP), it did not include activities related to CFES practice, especially civic engagement.
  - *Problems among high schools:* Gaining access and using the data were confusing for the schools.
  - *Good data for counseling, but not reporting:* The feedback from the one school that actually tried the data system indicated that the data were useful for individual counseling, but no attempt was made by the school to share reports with CFES. After the trial, CFES decided not to work with ESI.

- *Student surveys*: While my orientation is to utilize extant data when possible and use standardized surveys when data are not available, we found that neither approach worked well for CFES at that time. We developed and piloted a CFES student survey (see Case 4.4).

Engaged Research Supporting CFES
The partnership with CFES evolved during the period when I was writing about methods for engaged research; our shared agenda was driven by Rick Dalton's interests. To learn about his organization, I invited Dalton to UM to give a talk before deciding to perform the review summarized in Case 2.2. At that time, I developed an appreciation for the partnership model CFES used. One option he discussed with my students was doing a qualitative study of CFES students. In addition to the collaboration leading to the development and testing of surveys of student engagement (Case 4.2), Dalton invited us to collaborate on studies of urban and rural schools. I briefly summarize some of the insights gained from this process as an illustration of the evolution of the partnership.

Rural Schools
CFES is distinctive as a national network because of its commitment to rural schools; the opportunity to visit rural schools was interesting to both me and my graduate students. We visited four rural schools in two states and collaborated on a research paper with Dalton as an outcome of this process (Dalton, Bigelow, & St. John, 2012).

The interviews with students and adults yielded insights similar to findings about academic capital formation (ACF) in prior studies (St. John, Hu, & Fisher, 2011; Winkle-Wagner, Bowman, & St. John, 2012). We found a strong alignment between core practices in CFES and the social processes related to ACF (Table 3.1). Each core practice overlapped in a substantial way with the ACF process, with the exception of family uplift. The column on school contexts lists three other factors that emerged in the analysis of interviews as central to program success in these schools: capacity for change (C), selection process (S), and financial aid (FA).

In addition to being rural, each of the schools had a substantial *capacity for change* (C) as exemplified by the support given to CFES, which was vital to the role the core practices played in easing concerns about costs, building supportive networks, and providing trustworthy information. The formation of college knowledge and commitment to family uplift occurred as a result of core practices and, therefore, were only indirectly related to the capacity of the schools.

There were variations in the ways selection was implemented. CFES supports cohorts of at least 100 students in each urban school and leaves *selection* (S) to the schools, requesting only that they choose students who might not go to college without the additional support. Rural schools, often smaller than their urban counterparts, select at least 50 students, with some schools inviting the entire student population into the program and others selecting students across grade levels. The fact that schools select students for CFES makes it very difficult to generate any sort of comparison group for research on the effects of CFES on ACF.

It is evident from the analysis of focus groups that CFES provided support through mentoring that helped students develop navigational skills that would help them select and apply for college and student

TABLE 3.1
Alignment of CFES Core Practices and the Social Processes Related to Academic Capital Formation

CFES core practices *Academic capital formation*	*School contexts* • Capacity (C) • Selection (S) • Financial aid (FA)	*Pathways*	*Mentoring*	*Leadership*
Concerns about costs	S, C, FA	X	X	X
Supportive networks	C	X	X	X
Trustworthy information	S, C	X	X	X
College knowledge	Student outcome	X	X	X
Family uplift	Not evident	?	?	?

Note. X denotes overlap; ? denotes uncertain finding.
Source. Dalton, Bigelow, and St. John (2012, p. 200).

aid. The mentoring, college visits, and leadership all played substantial roles in changing student orientation toward college. In particular, it was evident that students developed personal and shared college knowledge. The shared knowledge was socially constructed among students, as evident in some of the sequences of comments within focus groups: mentoring among students created a strong culture in the schools; the mentoring of students by teachers created trustworthiness with adults in the schools, who provided a network that reinforced college aspirations; and leadership conferences enabled students to develop skills that could help in the navigation of new social environments in college. We found no evidence about family uplift in this study, but we focused more directly on this question in the follow-up study in urban schools.

Reflective Questions

The Editors

1. How did the process of trying different approaches to assessment and evaluation inform CFS?
2. What unique challenges do regional, state, and local networks face as they try to develop systemic accountability?
3. How do challenges facing rural schools differ from those in urban schools districts?

Case 3.3
Organizing the Detroit Consortium

Leanne Kang

In an effort to improve the percentage of college-prepared high school students, Michigan began a transition to higher graduation standards in 2006, requiring students to complete courses aligned with college enrollment, including Algebra II, by 2011. This requirement had a profound impact on schools serving low-income students: educators in both high schools and neighboring universities were faced with new opportunities and challenges. With no state support for professional development during the transition, along with lower levels of per student funding from the state and a declining population, schools serving low-income students found themselves ill prepared for the transition. In 2009, only 49% of Michigan students passed the Michigan Merit Exam (MME) in math. The Detroit Schools–Higher Education Consortium (DS-HEC; also referred to in this case as the consortium) was formed to bring university support to education reforms in Detroit. This case describes the development of the consortium.

Development of the Detroit Consortium

In Detroit, high school student test scores were abysmal, as were the rates of high school graduation and college enrollment. The state's policy to raise high school graduation standards and its effects on students in Detroit drew serious concern from higher education institutions in southeastern Michigan, especially those who had been working for years to improve the high school-to-college pipeline for historically underserved students.

Detroit had entered a particularly turbulent period in which financial deficits resulted in the governor appointing an emergency financial manager (EFM) to handle the school district's financial concerns. Meanwhile, a new system of charters proliferated throughout the city and the state, forcing the closure of hundreds of traditional schools in Detroit Public Schools (DPS) and the transfer of thousands of students.

These concerns prompted several individuals from the University of Michigan (UM Team) in 2008 to begin discussing how institutions of higher education—who had been committed to outreach efforts in Detroit for years—could come together to address the critical new challenges that DPS was facing.

The Development Phase

The DS-HEC began with several conversations between key individuals who had been working on increasing college access in Detroit and in other cities for decades. As assistant dean in the School of Education at UM, Henry Meares was responsible for special projects relating to K–16 relations, which for him entailed a deeper partnership with DPS. However, historically DPS had been distrustful of the university and often remained at a distance. Meares sought to bring the university and the school district together through his colleague, Tyrone Winfrey, who uniquely represented both DPS and the university as associate director of the UM Office of Undergraduate Admissions and vice president of the DPS school board. For several years, Meares and Winfrey discussed how their collective work could improve the high school to college pipeline in Detroit, beginning with developing trusting relationships. This resulted in an unprecedented move. The district's Education Committee welcomed Meares as its first member from the university.

In April 2009, educational leaders from DPS, Michigan State University (MSU), Wayne State University (WSU), and University of Detroit Mercy (UDM) agreed that the concerns in Detroit were great, having recently garnered the attention of the federal government. Conditions were ripe for institutional collaboration, and the representatives began to visualize what their collective impact could be. There was a shared sense that the consortium could act as an anchor for DPS as the school district weathered a swirl of policy initiatives and various efforts to dramatically reform education.

The Planning Grant
After the successful meeting with educational leaders across DPS and institutions of higher education, Meares and Ed St. John—as coprincipal investigators—set out to draft a proposal to the Ford Foundation for a planning grant to initiate the consortium. At the time, the Ford Foundation was interested in funding advocacy of children through community partnerships, which matched the consortium's goal of collaboration across institutions, but Meares and St. John also envisioned that future expansion would include membership from community-based groups. St. John provided a vision for a strong research arm of the consortium that would not only garner funding support from the Ford Foundation and beyond but also build capacity for collaboration and future work. In essence, they proposed an advocacy organization for the revitalization of Detroit's schools via the research capacity of the higher education institutions in southeastern Michigan; the consortium could have an important role in providing research to support the movement toward the bold new objectives being set for the DPS and their students.

The key piece in the planning grant was using an action inquiry model (AIM) St. John had already used and tested in a project in Indiana (St. John & Musoba, 2010) with three phases: *assessment*, which informs an *organizing* process and formation of *engaged research* projects. The planning grant would support the consortium as it established a governing structure and completed a baseline assessment of 9–16 pathways for preparation and college enrollment of DPS students.

The Governing Structure
The proposal for the planning grant was submitted in May 2010, revised in August, and accepted in December. Early in 2011, a subcommittee began drafting a memorandum of understanding (MOU) regarding the handling of data (access, usage, and reporting) between the DPS and the consortium. The MOU, however, would not be signed by DPS administrators until nearly two years later, significantly delaying what the consortium had outlined for the Ford Foundation.

While St. John grappled with the delay in attaining data, the consortium's steering committee worked on conceptualizing a governing structure and creating the mission and vision of the organization. The steering committee spent several months investigating other consortia models, like the Institute on Education Law and Policy in Newark and the Consortium on Chicago School Research, searching for critical lessons on structure, process, and sustaining a large agenda. The consortium quickly recognized their uniqueness in that they would be the first university-district partnership across seven institutions of higher education. Organizationally, it was imperative to become familiar with each institution's work and commitment in Detroit. The steering committee set out to develop a database and pinpoint areas of collaboration.

The steering committee also developed working groups, agreed on a membership fee, and outlined the following three goals of the consortium:

1. Contribute to and disseminate research that informs effective teaching/learning practices and policies for student college readiness.
2. Assist in transforming local school cultures to ensure college readiness and global competitiveness through systematic implementation of effective practices.
3. Advocate for effective, high-quality professional preparation and learning for teachers, administrators, and staff.

Confronting Challenges

In spite of the delay in obtaining the DPS data on high school cohorts, St. John and his team began to tackle some of the research goals articulated in the planning grant by looking at census data across Detroit neighborhoods to make some inferences about the social capital surrounding schools. Meanwhile, the consortium, by virtue of its monthly meetings and using its informal networks as a resource, managed to gather enough momentum that by 2012 membership expanded to include community entities such as Excellent Schools Detroit (ESD), Data-Driven Detroit, United Way, and Wayne State Regional Educational Service Agency (RESA).

St. John and Meares faced the challenge of asking for an extension of the planning grant from Ford without a report because of the lack of data.[1] This was particularly difficult because in 2012 the foundation's funding mission began to change significantly. Without data, the consortium continued to face the challenge of defining who they were and what they were committed to do. This was difficult in the face of reform initiatives turning over very quickly in Detroit, resulting in myriad shifting issues regarding the improvement of education. St. John argued that it was possible to fold Ford Foundation's new theme of More and Better Learning Time (MBLT) by conceptualizing its relationship to increasing college access. He suggested restructuring the working groups around mini grants for expanded learning or MBLT, coordination of university outreach, and development of a database. Still, many members of the consortium resisted Ford's new direction and debated about finding a new funding source. The strong research arm of the consortium had yet to come to fruition because the DPS had yet to sign and agree with the MOU.

Finally, in December 2012, the DPS signed the MOU. In 2013, armed with the DPS 2005–2009 student cohort data, St. John moved forward with the baseline assessment. Combining his previous work with the census data, the study evolved into work on the impact of community resources on educational opportunities in Detroit. The mixed-methods study used core concepts from econometric theories (e.g., the role of poverty on educational outcomes), theories of attainment (e.g., the role of completion of certain courses on graduation rates), and theories of social capital formation as a theoretical base. The report to Ford concluded that community-based resources can make a difference in student success and should play an integral role in education reform strategies. The report argued that the consortium had the potential to access community-based resources through its collaborative partnerships to improve educational opportunity for students in Detroit.

The consortium also organized a mini grant competition, inviting proposals from research teams engaged or interested in Detroit-based work; more than half of the capacity-building grant was set aside for funding these projects. The mini grant effort was a demonstration of the collective research power of multiple institutions of higher education and the potential of a research collaborative. The following three proposals were funded:

1. *High School Summer Program Incorporating Urban Debate League (Michigan State University).* MSU conducted and evaluated a six-week pilot of Urban Debate League–based support for 30 Detroit high school students. The study suggested that expanding multiple after-school settings and incorporating school day coursework could address college readiness and Common Core State Standards (CCSS) literacy requirements.
2. *Loyola High School Program Developing College Knowledge (Wayne State University).* WSU adapted KnowHow2GO materials to design, pilot, and assess the effectiveness of a blended learning course (online and face-to-face) teaching "college knowledge" to 10th-, 11th-, and 12th-grade students, primarily African American males, at Detroit's Loyola High School.
3. *Research and Action Partnership With Covenant House Academies (Michigan State University).* MSU initiated a partnership with Covenant House Michigan conducting baseline research of its three Covenant House Academies (CHA)—charter schools established in various parts of the city to meet the needs of homeless, runaway, and at-risk youth in Detroit.

While the baseline report was completed by mid-2013 and the summary shared with the Ford Foundation, their funded projects focused on evidence of extended learning. Thus, it became increasingly clear that Ford would fund a second phase only if there was a significant commitment to extended learning. In 2014 the foundation appointed a new president who will likely bring a new funding agenda. The mini grants, however, helped sustain momentum and demonstrated the research capacity of the consortium.

Conclusion

The development of the consortium is a lesson on how informal partnerships based on preexisting commitments to improve the high school–to–college pipeline enabled the founders to organize and leverage resources that led to collaboration. Their shared sense of concern for Detroit students and families also built the trust necessary for DPS to agree to a university-school partnership. This makes the consortium unique—the sharing of school district data is unprecedented.

> **Reflective Questions**
> The Editors
>
> 1. How did the interests of partner universities and public schools influence the development of the consortium?
> 2. How did political forces in the school system and university partners influence the organizing process in Detroit?
> 3. How did the state's oversight influence the organizing process in Detroit?
> 4. How can the partners deal better with political forces as they seek to build the consortium?
> 5. How well did the interests of partners coalesce, and how were conflicting interests resolved?
> 6. What role did trust or lack of trust play in promoting opportunity for students?
> 7. In spite of the obstacles, what did the consortium accomplish?
> 8. What do the experiences in Detroit suggest might be obstacles in your local context, and how is your context different?

Note

1. Funds from the planning grant, however, had been set aside to hire a postdoctoral researcher who could complete the assessment once data was provided.

4

USING INFORMATION FOR CHANGE

Guidance 4: Using Information for Change

1. *Align scholarship and action strategies*: Graduate students can learn about engaged scholarship by working with change advocates who have shared interests. The cases illustrate a range of student projects.
2. *Encourage exchange through engaged scholarship*: Both scholars and change advocates benefit from discussion and analysis. Cases of schools, classrooms, community organizations, and government agencies illustrate how researchers and projections learn together about educational initiatives for improving educational opportunities.
3. *View learning for change as an interactive process*: Engaged scholarship can shift the focus from documenting groups that fail to developing reforms that expand opportunity and promote success. The cases illustrate diverse means of learning from the experiences of students, practitioners, and change agents.

Action inquiry provides a mechanism for informing policy decisions and engaging in organizational learning. When practitioners are open to reflecting on information about learning outcomes, engaged research can inform policy development at all levels in educational systems as well as practitioners' perceptions regarding tactics and strategies and their navigation through the politics of educational change. Action inquiry helps participants learn about the barriers to change, disseminate information about these barriers, and collectively engage in the change processes that support student success. In this chapter, we provide an overview of the inquiry process, with a focus on strategies for using information to support and inform change processes. The cases illustrate some ways researchers can work in support of change:

- *Case 4.1: Student Tracking: Graduation of DC TAG Recipients* provides a summary of a study developed for the Washington, DC, government along with comments on the uses of the research.
- *Case 4.2: Surveys: CFES Pilot Study* discusses the development and use of student surveys within a national network of schools and colleges engaged in promoting college access.
- *Case 4.3: Student Interviews: Center for Student Advocacy* outlines a graduate student's project as a community organizer.
- *Case 4.4: Practitioner Interviews: Integrating Advanced Math Courses Into Urban Schools* describes how a graduate student's study informs interventionists providing support for urban educators.

We encourage readers to use the cases to consider how they can work with researchers to support and inform their efforts to improve educational opportunity. As action steps, we encourage researchers to consider how student tracking data, surveys, and studies of practices can help them in their efforts to expand educational opportunity.

Guide for Action

While action inquiry is conceptualized as a sequential process with a beginning and an ending demarcated by an evaluation, reformers must recognize how research and advocacy are used in organizations and policy decisions by government agencies. This chapter provides an introduction to action inquiry as a systemic process and concludes with a discussion of the uses of inquiry in policy, networks, and practice.

The Action Inquiry Process

Using action inquiry brings a learning orientation to educational reform. Integration of engaged research provides an alternative to merely using accountability reports on programs to inform change. Systemic uses of information tend to reinforce inequalities embedded in educational systems; change agents can use research to focus on identifying barriers and remedies. For the partner organizations, integration of research into action initiatives provides a means of coordinating bottom-up change with formal strategic planning and management in educational systems. This introduction to action inquiry focuses on starting new initiatives but can also be used to integrate engaged research into ongoing projects to revitalize them.

- *Build an understanding of the challenge.* When a new work group is formed, members should take time to familiarize themselves with the accountability reports, planning reports, and research used to identify a challenge and organize their group. In addition, the newly formed group should loop back through the steps of assessment, focusing on their own process of taking stock of the challenge. They should pay attention to the root causes of problems as a necessary step before considering how their work can be better aligned and the types of new or refined interventions needed to reduce gaps in opportunity. Begin the process with questions like the following:

    o What are the causes of the inequality, and how does the current system address it?
    o What solutions have been tried in the past, and how well did they work?
    o What aspects of the challenge have not been adequately addressed?
    o What aspects of the challenge require more study? For example, should you start with evaluation of current interventions?
    o What are your hypotheses about the causes of the challenges (reflective theory of change)?
    o Do the explanations hold up after using data to test the hypotheses?

- *Look internally and externally for solutions.* Talk with people in the organizations and communities involved. Get their perspectives on how they have addressed related challenges in the past. Educators, other professionals, and activists are frequently involved in professional organizations that study issues related to preparation, outreach support of academic transitions to college, retention, professional development, and other critical challenges facing colleges and universities. Read the literature on best practices and related subjects. We have found that practitioners develop their theories of action—their assumed ideas about how practice relates to student outcome—based on their experiences, possibly supplemented by reading literature. Many of the practices required in common core standards or in the literature on higher education are based on research, but the literature on best practices often has not tested the recommended practices in many of the contexts now required. In this volume, we have included case studies that actually tested the theories of change held by partners who used this research. Using this method, we hope to illustrate how theories of change can be informed through using research in an action inquiry process.

- *Assess possible solutions.* Consider alternatives in relation to the understanding of the problem developed in the first item of this list, *build an understanding of the challenge.* Action research involves experiments in actionable situations through tightly coupling evaluative research with the development of new initiatives. View prospective changes in practice as action experiments that can help build a deeper understanding of professional practice. When assessing possible interventions, consider the following:

    o Will the potential solutions address the challenge at your campus?
    o Do you need more data?
    o How can the solution be pilot tested? If you tried the solution, how would you know if it worked?
    o What information would you need to collect to know how well it worked?

- *Develop action plans.* Action plans should identify remedies that can be pilot tested and solutions that, if possible, can be implemented by current staff. If additional costs cannot be avoided, develop budgets for consideration internally and externally. (Remember that seeking additional funds can slow down the change process.) Develop action plans with time frames for implementation and evaluation. The plans for action experiments should take into consideration the design of the project, methods for implementation, people responsible for activities in the implementation, and an evaluation plan. Action planning by work groups can inform the strategic change process and adaptations of projects within partner organizations as they move forward.

The design of action plans and experiments is a critical aspect of the action inquiry process. Well-designed action experiments can be documented in ways that enable practitioners to communicate their findings to potential funding agencies, both internal and external. It is critical that plans for action experiments include designs for evaluation along with plans for the pilot test, another core element of action research. Well-designed experiments can be published in journals on teaching in all fields. Engaging faculty and professionals in the process of testing alternative solutions through action experiments can enhance the level and quality of discourse in departments and professional units. An experimental attitude also helps overcome the natural inclination to institutionalize a program that may or may not be meeting the goals it was designed to address and keeps practitioners open to revision.

Practice
Review formal and informal decision processes

Education organizations have formal planning, budgeting, and accountability processes; unfortunately, they typically do not reinforce efforts to reduce inequality or shrink gaps in opportunity and achievement for underrepresented students. Review decision processes to identify opportunities to use targeted studies and evaluation to promote organizational learning about strategies for promoting equity.

Alignment of Action Inquiry and Action Research

As policymakers and practitioners engage in action inquiry as a reflective process, they begin to see how they can use targeted research and evaluation studies to inform their actions as advocates for students. Each step of the action inquiry process can align with research projects to support professional and organizational learning (Table 4.1). Action research conducted by practitioners may be feasible in many instances, especially when the research can be used for a master's thesis or doctoral dissertation. Several of the cases in this volume started as class projects by graduate students. Researchers and educational partners need to consider what is feasible and move past narrowly defined boundaries of evaluation to action projects that test new strategies part of the change process. The following tasks should be undertaken as part of engaged research:

- Define the research/evaluation questions and coordinate with the AIM project's overall evaluation.
- Select a research design option.
- Choose a data collection method and collect the data.
- Analyze the data.
- Disseminate the results to campus planning groups and possibly a wider audience.
- Use evaluation results in an inquiry process to fully implement, alter and implement, or not implement the pilot-tested intervention.

To start aligning research with action inquiry involves thinking through how different types of information and analysis can be used to inform action. We encourage the following:

- Use student tracking data for the analysis of the educational progress of diverse groups and evaluating the effects of programs and interventions on promoting achievement and attainment while reducing inequality.
- Use surveys to build understanding of the effectiveness of interventions, including the ways student engagement promotes higher aspirations and attainment for underrepresented students.
- Use interviews and focus groups to build understanding of the barriers to change within the system.

Use Student Tracking Data

Student tracking data have become a new gold standard for research supporting educational reform because it is possible to track all students, overcoming problems associated with selection of students for interventions and control groups. Even when randomization is used to test a new intervention, it is crucial to track all students because students invited into an intervention may opt in or out due to social and economic factors out of the control of interventionists and researchers.

Practice
Investigate the student data available and
how they can be used

The information technology used in education is making it easier to use analysis of student tracking data as part of action inquiry. Specifically consider the following questions:

- What pathways do students travel as they move through your educational system, and what information is retained?
- What access do you and research partners have to these existing data sources, providing appropriate protections for human subjects?
- How can available existing data be used in targeted assessment studies to identify barriers and/or evaluation studies that can help you identify interventions or refine practices (see Table 4.1)?

The availability of existing data to some extent determines what questions can be answered. Most tracking data systems have extremely limited types of information. Protection of human subjects makes it extremely difficult to access student records in many instances. Combining new data, including interviews, with existing data can provide better information for evaluation.

Use Surveys

Consider how surveys might provide additional sources of information to inform practice. The classic research design in psychology, sociology, and education involves some observations or surveys for treatment and control

TABLE 4.1
Role of Research and Evaluation in Action Inquiry

Stages	Action inquiry tasks	Roles of engaged researchers
Stage 1: Assess	• Identify possible challenges • Collect and analyze data • Prioritize challenges • Organize work groups	• Identify critical success indicators (CSIs) related to achievement and attainment by diverse groups (based on income, race, prior preparation, etc.)
Stage 2: Organize	• Coordinate budgeting to provide necessary support • Find an appropriate research partner • Coordinate inquiry with campus planning and budgeting	• Identify barriers and alternative strategies to address them

Stage 3: Take Action	• Each campus workgroup engages in a process to do the following:
	  Build an understanding of the challenge
	  Look internally and externally for solutions
	  Assess possible solutions
	  Develop action plans
	  Implement a pilot test and evaluate results
		• Design interventions and evaluations

Stage 4: Evaluate	• Involve research partners in evaluation and analysis of outcomes • Have campus teams coordinate implementation and evaluation, providing reviews of plans, encouraging presentations to campus planning groups, and facilitating coordination of the inquiry process with campus planning	• Use evaluation methods that provide information about critical success indicators • Consider implications for planning, budgeting, and practice in future years

> **Practice**
> **Consider when and how student surveys might inform decisions about policy and practice**
>
> Case 4.2 illustrates a step in the process of developing surveys that can be used in engaged research informing practice, as well as for accountability and evaluation. Review the case and consider the following questions:
>
> - When are new survey instruments needed and, if necessary, how can they be used to support organizational development and educational practice?
> - How do the patterns of student engagement inform your efforts to provide support for students underrepresented among college graduates?
> - How well did the development and use of surveys meet the information needs identified in the assessment? (Also look back at Case 2.2.)

groups, both randomly assigned, which is also the standard for evaluation research. However, in education it is usually not possible to achieve this standard because: (a) interventionists usually don't want to randomly assign benefits; and (b) regardless of whether a control group is randomly selected, it is often difficult to motivate members to respond if they did not receive the intervention. National surveys of student engagement often have such low response rates that it is difficult to glean useful information about underrepresented groups, especially if they are not very engaged in academic and social processes. Surveys provide a useful method for identifying patterns of student engagement in interventions.

Use Student Interviews and Focus Groups

The public accountability systems used in K–12 and higher education usually include indicators that can be used for achievement and attainment, but frequently further analysis is required to: (a) identify gaps across racial and income groups; and (b) explore the relationships among factors that relate to outcomes. This requires "digging" into accountability reports (e.g., school report cards) and exploring how different structures and processes within schools relate to differences in outcomes. Research that tracks a cohort of students through the system (e.g., from middle school through high school graduation on to college entry and persistence) can be used to establish a baseline to examine challenges.

> **Practice**
> **Consider using student interviews conducted by an independent researcher**
>
> Research that captures students' perspectives can inform your efforts to expand opportunity. Interviews and focus groups provide a means of gaining insights that inform improvement in support services and student advocacy. Consider how independent interviews can inform policymakers about barriers to policy implementation and intervention. See Case 4.3 for an example.

Consider Practitioners' Perspectives

The implementation of new requirements has an impact on interactions between students and teachers. For example, the requirement that all students complete advanced math in Michigan was implemented without professional development for teachers. It is important to consider practitioners' perspectives and learning needs when they are required to change practice.

> **Practice**
> **Consider practitioners' perspectives**
>
> Case 4.4 illustrates how practitioner interviews can inform refinement of educational practice. Consider practitioners' perspectives when designing, implementing, and refining intervention strategies. To secure the authentic voices of educators engaged in implementing reforms, it is essential to ensure protection for human subjects so they won't experience retribution for their critiques, a form of information that is especially important to consider in the design of interventions.

Case 4.1

Student Tracking: Graduation of DC TAG Recipients

Amy S. Fisher and Rehva Jones McKinnon

We present findings from a study using student records in support of the DC Office of the State Superintendent of Education (OSSE). The agency had access to records but lacked the capability to use them to address policy questions from Congress. After developing a data agreement (Case 3.1), DC OSSE provided data to the research team at the University of Michigan. As the researcher on this project, Amy S. Fisher provided DC OSSE with a series of tables, plus a discussion of methods so they could use the information in their reports. In this chapter, Fisher discusses the analyses she completed, and Rehva Jones McKinnon discusses the uses of the research by the OSSE.

Summary Research Report

Amy S. Fisher

The DC OSSE began collecting data on students when the District of Columbia Tuition Assistance Grant (DC TAG) was funded in 2000. In preparation for the reauthorization of the DC TAG program after 10 years, OSSE sought an evaluation. To begin, we provided an analysis of completion rates by DC TAG recipients generated from OSSE records and data from the National Student Clearinghouse (NSC). The summary examines high schools with the highest college graduation rates of DC TAG recipients and colleges with the highest rates of graduation by DC TAG recipients.[1] (For ease of reading, tables are placed at the end of the case.)

The analyses used first-time, first-year college students enrolling initially in the fall terms of 2003, 2004, and 2005. We linked student data from OSSE's OneApp system with NSC information. A variable for historically Black colleges and universities (HBCUs) was generated by comparing lists of HBCUs with the college names provided by OneApp.

Each year more DC TAG grantees are female than male, but over time the gender gap narrowed (Figure 4.1). Less than 1% of DC TAG grantees had unknown gender in any given year. The graduation rate for the

80   USING ACTION INQUIRY IN ENGAGED RESEARCH

2003 cohort after six years (the time between when they graduated from high school and when the data were analyzed) was approximately 46% (Figure 4.2). After five years about 42% of the 2004 cohort of DC TAG participants graduated, and after four years the graduation rate of 2005

Figure 4.1. Percentage of DC TAG grantees whose gender is male, female, or unknown.

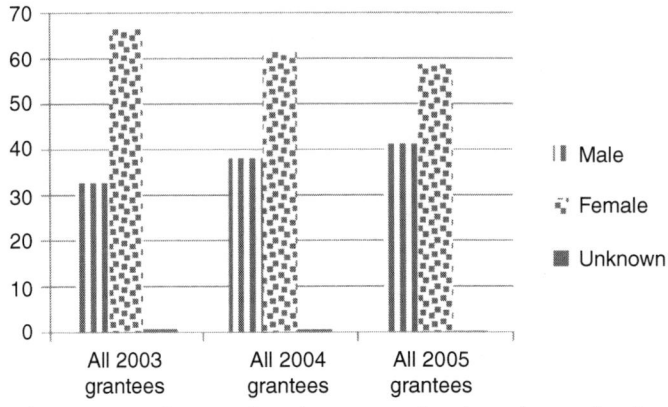

Note. This chart represents all grantees in a given year, not just those who were first-time, first-year students in that year.

Figure 4.2. Cumulative graduation rate (%) of the 2003, 2004, and 2005 DC TAG cohorts.

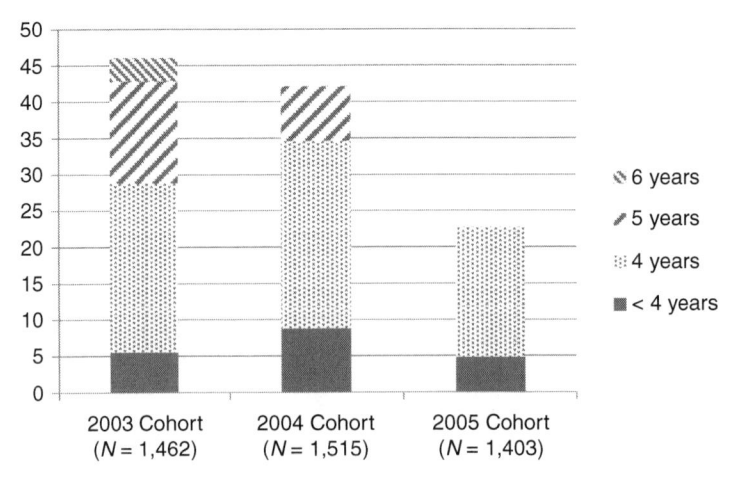

cohort DC TAG participants was approximately 23%. At the time of this analysis, five- and six-year graduation rates were not available for the 2004 and 2005 cohorts. The graduation rate across DC TAG cohorts going as far back as 2000 (i.e., students whose first year of college was between 2000 and 2005) is 43.8%.

High School Attended
For a better understanding of conditions earlier in the pipeline, we examined both the types of high schools DC TAG students attended and in which ward in the district they lived. DC TAG participants who graduated from private high schools had the highest college graduation rates among types of high schools (Table 4.2), and students who attended public schools graduated college at the second highest rate, followed by charter high schools.

DC TAG students who began at public or private institutions (either two-year or four-year, but not HBCUs) had the highest graduation rates after four, five, and six years (Table 4.3). The only exception was the 2004 cohort when proprietary institutions had the highest less-than-four-years graduation rate. In the other two cohorts, however, none of the students who first attended a proprietary college graduated. Across all three cohorts, there was great variation in the graduation rate of TAG grantees who first attended an HBCU. The cumulative four-year rate is highest for the 2004 cohort and lowest for the 2005 cohort; however, after five years, the graduation rate for the 2003 cohort exceeds that of the 2004 cohort.

Postsecondary Institutions
Discussed here are the types of colleges where DC TAG grantees began their postsecondary education and where it ended for those who had graduated by the time of the evaluation. By linking with the NSC data, it is also possible to see which specific postsecondary institutions were most attended by DC TAG grantees. Not surprisingly, the majority of the top 10 colleges or universities first attended by DC TAG grantees (across all three cohorts) are in the greater DC area (Table 4.4). When looking at the top 30 after combining the three cohorts, it is clear that the DC TAG program has made it possible for numerous district students to attend college out of state, across the country, as well as to enroll in a private institution within Washington, DC.

TABLE 4.2
DC TAG Graduates After Four, Five, and Six Years by High School Type

	Less than 4 years (%)	4 years		5 years		6 years	
		4 years (%)	Cumulative row (%)^	5 years (%)	Cumulative row (%)^	6 years (%)	Cumulative row (%)^
2003 cohort ($N = 1462$)							
DC public school ($n = 840$)	3.9	22.6	26.5	14.4	40.9	3.3	44.2
DC public charter ($n = 120$)	1.7	13.3	15.0	21.7	36.7	5.0	41.7
Private* ($n = 218$)	6.9	35.8	42.7	13.8	56.5	4.1	60.6
Other** ($n = 236$)	10.2	17.4	27.6	9.7	37.3	1.7	39.0
Missing ($n = 48$)	14.6	31.2	45.8	10.4	56.2	-	-
2004 cohort ($N = 1515$)							
DC public school ($n = 849$)	4.9	24.3	29.2	8.4	37.6	-	-
DC public charter ($n = 190$)	5.0	17.9	22.9	3.7	26.6	-	-
Private* ($n = 223$)	8.1	35.9	44.0	8.1	52.1	-	-
Other** ($n = 194$)	4.0	25.8	29.8	7.2	37.0	-	-

Missing (*n* = 59)	3.0	35.6	38.6	6.8	45.4	-	-
2005 cohort (*N* = 1403)							
DC public school (*n* = 725)	3.2	17.7	20.9	-	-	-	-
DC public charter (*n* = 202)	1.0	7.4	8.4	-	-	-	-
Private* (*n* = 221)	8.6	27.6	36.2	-	-	-	-
Other** (*n* = 197)	8.6	17.8	26.4	-	-	-	-
Missing (*n* = 58)	10.3	20.7	31.0	-	-	-	-

*Includes parochial.

**Includes GED, home school, and other.

^Cumulative row percentage reflects students who graduated in four years or less, five years or less, and six years or less.

TABLE 4.3
DC TAG Graduates After Four, Five, and Six Years by Type of First College Attended

	Less than 4 years (%)	4 years Graduated in 4 years (%)	Cumulative row (%)^	5 years Graduated in 5 years (%)	Cumulative row (%)^	6 years Graduate in 6 years(%)	Cumulative row (%)^
2003 cohort (*N* = 1462)							
Public/private HBCU (*n* = 518)	5.2	23.2	28.4	20.3	48.7	3.7	52.4
Public college (*n* = 449)	8.2	36.5	44.7	18.3	63.0	3.6	66.6
Private college (*n* = 137)	12.4	35.0	47.4	13.1	60.5	8.0	68.5
Proprietary college (*n* = 1)	0.0	0.0	0.0	0.0	0.0	0.0	0.0
Missing* (*n* = 357)	0.0	2.2	2.2	0.0	2.2	0.3	2.5
2004 cohort (*N* = 1515)							
Public/private HBCU (*n* = 466)	3.6	30.9	34.5	10.1	44.6	-	-
Public college (*n* = 530)	7.2	34.3	41.5	10.0	51.5	-	-
Private college (*n* = 140)	10.0	36.4	46.4	9.3	55.7	-	-

Proprietary college (n = 5)	40.0	0.0	40.0	0.0	40.0	-	-	-
Missing* (n = 374)	0.3	3.7	4.0	0.3	4.3	-	-	-
2005 cohort (N = 1403)								
Public/private HBCU (n = 368)	5.4	18.8	24.2	-	-	-	-	-
Public college (n = 490)	6.9	28.2	35.1	-	-	-	-	-
Private college (n = 136)	8.1	29.4	37.5	-	-	-	-	-
Proprietary college (n = 4)	0.0	0.0	0.0	-	-	-	-	-
Missing* (n = 405)	0.5	1.2	1.7	-	-	-	-	-

^Cumulative row percentages reflect students who graduated in four years or less, five years or less, and six years or less.

*Type of first college attended not listed in database.

TABLE 4.4
2003–2005 Cohort Graduation Rate Comparison at Most Attended Colleges*

	Name of college	DC TAG grantees	DC TAG graduation rate (%)	Institutional graduation rate (%)+
1.	Montgomery College	339	14.50	12.00
2.	North Carolina Agricultural and Technical State University	326	33.70	41.00
3.	Prince George's Community College	228	7.90	4.00
4.	Virginia State University	157	32.50	42.00
5.	Norfolk State University	106	23.60	31.00
6.	University of Maryland Eastern Shore	100	26.09	37.00
7.	George Washington University	99	47.50	78.00
8.	Bowie State University	98	24.50	37.00
9.	Howard University	92	48.90	69.00
10.	Temple University	85	49.40	60.00
11.	University of Maryland University College	85	0.00	4.00
12.	Delaware State University	81	29.60	37.00
13.	Johnson C. Smith University	80	41.20	42.00
14.	Virginia Commonwealth University	79	40.50	47.00
15.	North Carolina Central University	77	39.00	48.00
16.	University of Michigan	74	81.10	88.00

(Continues)

TABLE 4.4. (*Continued*)

	Name of college	DC TAG grantees	DC TAG graduation rate (%)	Institutional graduation rate (%)+
17.	Pennsylvania State University (The)	73	54.80	84.00
18.	Virginia Union University	60	25.00	25.00
19.	Florida Agricultural and Mechanical University	61	34.40	39.00
20.	Texas Southern University	57	0.00	12.00
21.	Fayetteville State University	55	21.80	36.00
22.	George Mason University	54	38.90	68.00
23.	Hampton University	53	54.70	54.00
24.	University of Maryland at College Park	50	100.00	80.00
25.	Northern Virginia Community College	46	2.20	13.00
26.	Cheney University of Pennsylvania	45	22.20	29.00
27.	University of Virginia	43	90.00	93.00
28.	University of Wisconsin–Madison	43	79.10	79.00
29.	Winston-Salem State University	43	37.20	45.00
30.	Georgetown University	41	61.00	93.00

*N of cohorts = 4380.
^Graduation rate is of students who started at these schools and includes those who graduated from the school where they started and those who graduated from schools they may have transferred to from these schools.
+Data come from the Integrated Postsecondary Education System (IPEDS) and reflect six-year graduation rates in 2007.

Use of DC TAG Data Analysis

Rehva Jones McKinnon

The final report was met with great enthusiasm by DC TAG staff because (a) for the first time, the program had graduation rates to report; (b) the data and analytics were strong and from a highly credible source; and (c) the shift in program focus from access to persistence was validated through the data. Close examination of the data by ward revealed opportunities for improvement. The data analysis of DC TAG graduation rates was used in the following ways:

1. In October 2009, DC TAG's 10-Year Accomplishments Report was completed, which included the graduation data (see osse .dc.gov/sites/default/files/dc/sites/osse/publication/attachments/ dctag-10-year-accomplishments-report.pdf).
2. On October 13, 2009, the OSSE dedicated a policy forum to present the program's 10-year accomplishments. The graduation data were front and center, serving as a catalyst for public discourse about college access and persistence.
3. In 2010, the high school feedback reports were generated based on the graduation data. The OSSE shared these reports with high school principals and their college access teams. These data "road shows" enabled high schools to refocus efforts on issues of college access and preparation.
4. In an effort to shift the district's focus from access to persistence and success, in January 2011, the OSSE hosted the district's first College Access Providers Conference, at Gallaudet University's Kellogg Conference Center.
5. In January 2011, the OSSE hosted a training session on financial aid for parents. In addition to presenting the graduation data, parents were provided with the guidance necessary to complete FAFSA and DC OneApp.

> **Reflective Questions**
> The Editors
>
> 1. How did the DC TAG program become the focus of the research study undertaken?
> 2. Why did the OSSE decide to follow through on this research project?
> 3. How did the OSSE use the research findings to advance the agency's agenda?
> 4. What aspects of the data analysis were most useful to DC TAG?
> 5. How much did the data analysis contribute to the shift from college access to college completion?
> 6. How did the politics of the DC case differ from the Detroit case (Case 3.3)?
> 7. What role did opportunities to collaborate on projects of mutual interest play in the DC project?
> 8. How does the baseline assessment in Detroit (Case 3.3) differ in intent from the DC study?
> 9. DC's consortium did not continue after the planning grant and it remains uncertain whether the Detroit project will continue. Given financial constraints, how might partnerships of this type be sustained without foundation funding?

Case 4.2
Surveys: CFES Pilot Study

*Ed St. John, Rick Dalton,
and Victoria J. Milazzo Bigelow*

From the start of the partnership with the UM Team, CFES had expressed interest in a survey of students. After trying out methods of collecting information using extant data (e.g., EMI, National Student Clearinghouse), we decided to test the survey method. This case illustrates the use of school surveys with a focus on one high school (Green) in comparison to the findings for the entire survey. As a conclusion, Rick Dalton comments on the next steps in the research.

Green High School as an Illustrative Case
Ed St. John and Victoria J. Milazzo Bigelow

Green High School attracts low-income students who aspire to complete college and find careers that uplift their families. We briefly look at how the Green respondents compare to the entire group of respondents to the CFES survey before examining how the cocurriculum strategy for college knowledge developed in the school. We also provide some analysis of interviews with students and teachers to illustrate the complementarity of quantitative and qualitative methods (using focus groups; see St. John et al. [2015] for study overview).

Green CFES Scholars
A total of 42 9th- and 10th-grade students responded to the survey. Green students were older than most of the other CFES respondents in 2014, who were in middle school (Table 4.5). Three-quarters of Green respondents were from low-income families eligible for federally subsidized lunch (Table 4.6), a higher rate of poverty than evident nationally for CFES. In addition, all respondents from Green were from a minority group, a further contrast to the CFES general population (Table 4.7). Further, Green respondents were from families with education levels similar to the CFES respondents overall; most were from families with either some college (26%) or four-year degrees (31%), illustrating the new pattern of urban poverty, in which many of those in poverty have education beyond high school. These students are clearly from families striving for cross-generation uplift, but parents' gains in educational attainment did not lift them out of poverty (Table 4.8).

Pathways to College and Careers
The challenges of developing a compelling theme to attract students and providing realistic information about college costs converged at Green. The school is a landing place for students in the option pool who are interested in education and for transfer students from closed schools or students who did not have a good experience at their original school. When the principal realized the admissions process was delivering students who hadn't chosen the school and weren't necessarily interested in the teaching theme, he

responded by adding the liberal arts academy to meet their needs; with this addition, students were able to explore a larger range of major options for college. For example, a student commented, "I think I want to get a degree in medicine—biology major or premed—or I want to do journalism. I haven't decided yet." The next student in the same focus group added, "I've always wanted to own my own business or actually travel the world and be like a hotel critic so you're getting paid to go on vacation." Clearly these students were still figuring out what they wanted, but they did not mention the school's teaching theme.

TABLE 4.5
Grade Levels of Green and All CFES Respondents

	Green (%)	All CFES (%)
6th grade	0	22
7th grade	0	26
8th grade	0	31
9th grade	62	12
10th grade	38	8
No response	0	0
Total N of respondents	42	940

Note. Totals may not sum to 100 due to rounding.

TABLE 4.6
Students Reporting Participation in Federal Free and Reduced Cost Lunch at Green Compared to All CFES Respondents

	Green (%)	All CFES (%)
Yes	76	64
No	14	25
Don't know	10	11
No response	0	0

TABLE 4.7
Race/Ethnicity of Green Students Compared to All CFES Respondents

	Green (%)	All CFES (%)
Caucasian or White, not Hispanic	0	40
Black or African American	31	21
American Indian or Alaska Native	0	1
Latino/a or Hispanic	48	14
Asian, Native Hawaiian, or Other Pacific Islander	14	18
No response	7	5

TABLE 4.8
Highest Education Levels of Students' Families for Green Students Compared to All CFES Students

	Green (%)	All CFES (%)
Did not finish high school	12	6
High school diploma or GED	10	16
Some college (community college, technical school, trade school)	26	25
Four-year degree (e.g., BA, BS) or higher	31	31
Don't know	21	23
No response	0	0

Teachers indicated family concerns about potential earnings were a factor in the addition of a general liberal arts theme, which would make it clear to families their children would have choices about majors and careers. The majority of both overall and Green respondents self-identified as CFES Scholars (Table 4.9). A very high percentage of the Green students knew about the courses and grades they would need for college, and virtually all knew about student financial aid.

TABLE 4.9
CFES Scholars Engagement in College/Career Pathways Practices for Green Students Compared to All CFES Respondents

	Green (%)	All CFES (%)
CFES Scholar (self-identify)	76	93
Talked to college student last year	57	71
College students visited my school last year	57	63
College representative visited last year	45	55
Visited college campus last year	57	79
Know about financial aid/scholarships	98	91
Know the courses I need for college	88	72
Talk with my family about college	83	81
Need to improve grades for best college	98	92

Students described their involvement in CFES as a process of "joining" the group. One student said, "I heard about it my freshman year. I actually had [teacher's name] for my life skills class. So in the life skills class he said, 'You're a good student, you should join CFES.' So once I joined I went on college trips." The activities through CFES gave students opportunities to learn about career paths. While some students used their involvement to broaden their interests, as the foregoing student's comments illustrate, others found their interest in teaching was intensified through their involvement. For example, another Green student reflected, "I want to be a first-grade, elementary school teacher. I want to go to college. I really do."

About two-thirds of overall and Green respondents indicated they planned to go to a four-year college after high school (Table 4.10), but a higher percentage of Green students either didn't know their plans or had more than one response (e.g., work and college).

An overarching concern at Green was that both students and their parents wanted to learn about college options. As expressed by one teacher, students and parents had concerns about costs: "They're aware that there

TABLE 4.10
Green Students' Plans After High School Compared to All CFES Respondents

	Green (%)	All CFES (%)
Go to work	2	6
Go to a trade or technical school	0	2
Attend a two-year or community college	0	7
Attend a four-year college or university	67	65
Don't know, more than one response, or no response	31	21

Note. Totals may not sum to 100 due to rounding.

are scholarship opportunities out there, but they don't have the confidence to know that, 'I can get that.'" Green teachers recognized that students had to work through personal challenges to have an opportunity to attend a good four-year program and that high grades would help them earn grant and/or scholarship funding. Finding realistic pathways for students was a critical concern for teachers and administrators at Green:

> We always try to set up meetings, you know, we've had in the past, we've had our guidance counselor, our senior adviser come and do a presentation about the FAFSA and talk to kids about financial aid and scholarship opportunities. But for the most part it's something that we definitely need to work and focus more on, because financial aid is a huge issue.

Engagement in CFES Social Support
The social support provided through CFES is more comprehensive than that provided by most school-college networks. Two-thirds of Green students were acquainted with college dropouts, a higher percentage than for all CFES respondents (Table 4.11). Students reported having either adult or student mentors and that their mentors engaged them in talking about college. Most found it easy to talk with their mentors.

The CFES program director at Green described his approach to working with colleges:

We always have, you know, sessions where somebody will come in and they'll explain, you know, the admissions process, they'll talk about financial aid, they give a run-down on basically all aspects of what the kids would need to know for college and you know we bring all kids there. We bring freshmen, sophomores, juniors, and seniors.

TABLE 4.11
CFES Scholar Engagement in Mentoring and Social Support for Green Students Compared to All CFES Respondents

	Green (%)	*All CFES (%)*
I know students who dropped out of college	67	51
Talked with older student about problems	48	38
Older student is a mentor	50	42
Adult mentor (teacher, counselor, other)	43	63
Mentor makes it easy to ask questions	71	72
Teachers encourage college plans	83	88
Mentor encourages me to think about college	81	74
I am a mentor	10	45

He tried to build ongoing partnerships with colleges: "Every time I try to set up a visit I tell them, like, 'Listen, trust me, you want freshmen, you want sophomores,' because those kids, especially these inner-city kids, they go to that campus, it's the first one they've ever seen, that sticks in their mind."

Leadership Through Service
The Green leadership team realized they could build on community connectivity as they addressed students' concerns about college costs (Table 4.12). For example, a teacher reflected on the factors that attracted students to the school:

We have a really good community base where the teacher-student rapport has always been very strong at our school so, you know, a lot of times you'll find siblings, you know, brothers and sisters coming to the school because they know the good opportunities that have been offered for their brothers and sisters.

TABLE 4.12
Student Involvement in Engaged Leadership Practices Comparing Green and All CFES Respondents

	Green (%)	*All CFES (%)*
Involved in service activities	45	47
Played on a sport team	10	47
Students seek my opinion	88	78
See self as a leader	81	80
Band/chorus	5	45
Community service through school	74	76
Worked with other students on out-of-class projects	67	62
Worked with other students to solve problems	59	68
Served as a mentor or coach to younger students	13	40
Organized activities for student groups	21	30
Learned about project planning and team work	69	59

A student observed, "We also go to an elementary school once a year and teach kids about college to start off. We do activities with them like face painting. We read to them and we feed them stuff." Volunteering in lower-grade schools was commonly practiced. Events and activities were often organized by students and helped them build awareness of community and social issues as an integral part of their high school education, at the same time providing experiences aligned with criteria considered in college admission. Social networking provides students with an opportunity to learn from each other, a key skill for group cooperative learning in college. There was also a cross-grade approach to student leadership illustrated by the relatively high percentage of Green students who had older students as mentors and who talked with older students about their problems.

Teachers and administrators helped students consider specific challenges they would face. For example, one Green teacher expressed a sentiment widely echoed across interviews: "I know in the past, even recently, one of our best students, our most hard-working students, top five in the class—she was undocumented, and she wasn't even able to apply for the Posse scholarship, which she very well could have won." To work through this barrier, Green teachers informed undocumented immigrant students they could receive college credits through the City University of New York system.

Next Steps

Rick Dalton

The pilot test of the surveys illustrated their utility for accountability purposes and their potential for supporting schools in their CFES projects and informing broader school improvement efforts. A summary of decisions regarding recommendations on next steps in the survey process follows:

- *School-based strategy*

    o *Recommendation:* CFES has an array of models (school-wide, cohort groups, etc.), and schools are engaged in a variety of reform initiatives. St. John proposed constructing a tool kit for schools that would provide them with options about using the surveys.
    o *Status:* We hoped to pilot test this during the 2014–2015 school year, but we have delayed this at least a year because the process seems too burdensome for our schools.

- *Option for fall and spring surveys*

    o *Recommendation:* Since there were substantial changes in student engagement during the year, we proposed and CFES agreed to give schools the option of conducting both fall and spring surveys.

- *Status:* In the 2015–2016 school year, schools may have that option and will be provided with a report on the changes that occurred during the school year.

- *High school surveys*

    - *Recommendation:* Since the outset of this initiative, the goal has been to develop CFES surveys for high school students with questions about college application and choice processes.
    - *Status:* We decided to add 10th graders in the spring 2014 surveys. We will explore further options in the future.

Reflective Questions
The Editors

1. How might further development of surveys provide a mechanism for accountability in schools and colleges in the CFES network?
2. How might accountability research generated from surveys of CFES scholars inform other groups and organizations involved in school-college networks?
3. How does the practice of sharing results of research in publications for practitioners and researchers differ from traditional program evaluation?
4. What do researchers, schools, and colleges gain from collaborating on research ventures?
5. What practices did the program leaders consider important to the students' success based on the research conducted?
6. Collecting new data over using existing data is time-consuming. In this example, did the surveys have a substantial enough impact to merit their continuation or expansion?
7. What would be the benefits and drawbacks of surveying students in your context?

Case 4.3
Student Interviews: Center for Student Advocacy

Anna Chiang and Wesley Ganson

This case provides a summative report by a graduate student researcher on interviews with middle school students from two schools that were involved in a mentoring program. It also includes comments by Wesley Ganson, organizer of the mentoring program and director of the Center for Student Advocacy.

Students' Experiences in Mentoring Programs

Anna Chiang

For the past three years the Center for Student Advocacy has pilot tested a comprehensive mentoring program at two schools in Detroit: Fredrick Douglass, a K–12 school for boys; and Detroit International Academy, a K–12 school for girls. Known as "Boys to Men" at Fredrick Douglass and "Ladies of Distinction" at Detroit International Academy, the comprehensive mentoring program focuses on academic preparation for at-risk middle school students with the intent to work with them through middle school and on through high school graduation. Thirty students were selected to participate in this program (15 girls and 15 boys); the students who were selected tend to have a history of behavioral problems, were held back academically, were older than their peers when they entered middle school, and/or had low grade point averages (a 2.0 average for the group).

The comprehensive mentoring program comprises two major components: mentorship and tutoring. The mentorship component focuses on the development of student aspirations, goal setting, navigational skills, and building knowledge of college through college visits and one-on-one mentoring by volunteer college students. The tutoring component tutors students in basic literacy and math. The program also focuses on extending opportunities for individual and group learning.

Our interviews focused on the following question: How has the program impacted students' academic and social development? The focus group interviews were conducted at the respective academies during the mentorship program sessions. Focus group interviews for both Boys to

Men and Ladies of Distinction were 60 minutes long; the staff interviews at both schools lasted 30 to 45 minutes.

Emergent Themes
Prior to joining the program, most of the students from both schools had no awareness of the purpose of their involvement. Students from both programs indicated either that they had been "automatically chosen" or they chose to join through an invitation from staff or friends. One focus group respondent commented, "The program will help you with your grades and kind of keep you out of trouble and keep your head on strong." Another student from Ladies of Distinction had a different perception of the program. She recalled "When I first heard about the program, I thought it was like anger management or something." The majority of the students had no prior expectations about their involvement or the potential level of impact on their individual academic and social development. The following four salient categories emerged to assess program impact:

1. Academic achievement
2. College knowledge
3. Mentorship
4. Community exposure

Academic Achievement
The students selected for this program were considered to be "at risk" at their schools. In order to address the students' academic concerns and assist them in achieving their academic potential, the Center for Student Advocacy created a curriculum that incorporated tutoring, mentorship, and individualized student action plans (ISAP) for academic goal setting. Weekly meetings consisted of tutoring sessions, group check-ins, and individual progress reports to identify strengths and weaknesses in their academic plans.

Students spoke at length about their perception of their academic status prior to joining the program and the progress they have made since being involved. One female student commented, "When we first started out it wasn't going so great with our grades. But in the group, all of our grades have improved and increased over time. When we do our sessions, we say what we want to improve and we work on it as a team and it actually improves." Another female student expressed the significant impact the program had on their academic progress:

> It was this one day when we had to show our report cards [to the program director]. We were just sitting there, like . . . man, I don't know how my report card looks. . . . When we went there and looked at our report cards we were like, "It was better than last year." We were so surprised! Oh, my goodness, we were so geeked. We still could improve and do better but that was actually cool. We jumped from a C to an A, an F to a B. We was [sic] like so happy that we did something cool and educational at the same time. And we actually learned from that, that it's not impossible.

The curriculum in the program helped students gain confidence in their academic ability. More importantly, the academic rigor and continuous support they received from the program helped the students actualize their potential—to reach goals they would not have reached on their own.

The male students expressed similar sentiments about the growth in their self-confidence and academic potential after being involved in the program. One student, in particular, recalled,

> You know when I first went here I didn't really have a goal. . . . I just wanted to go to school and get it over with. When I got to this program and, like, since I've been getting good grades, you have to keep a goal. I'm trying to get a 4.0 or a 3.5 or higher. I never knew about valedictorian and so one day my teacher came to me and told me I was going to be valedictorian. I said I didn't know what it was.

Perceptions of self-actualization of academic potential were common in both groups. These students not only removed themselves from being at risk but also strived to reach their highest potential.

College Knowledge

Most of the students entered the program with a lack of college knowledge and exposure to the various options beyond high school. *College knowledge*, as defined by Mattern and Shaw (2010), is the information students need to enable them to apply to and attend college. Most students involved in this program did not imagine college to be a feasible option, considering their academic circumstances (e.g., academic probation, low GPA). Since attaining a postsecondary degree is increasingly vital in today's society, the program made it a priority to increase college knowledge among its students.

One of the ways the program sought to promote a college-going culture was by exposing the students to college through activities such as college visits. A student from Ladies of Distinction talked about her experience with these college trips:

> It kind of impacted me personally because I don't know exactly if I want to stay in a dorm or stay at home, how the classroom is going to be like, . . . how the dorm rooms will look like and how the bathrooms and everything, where you eat, how you get a job, go to store and just like regular things.

As conveyed by this student, attending these college trips helped the students visualize their life on a college campus, which might not have been possible without the program. Through various college exposures, students who had not previously thought about attending college realized it was possible. One of the male students commented,

> I really didn't plan on having a goal to go to college or nothing. I was trying to get school over with quick. I used to skip school a lot. I used to hang with my cousins; we used to do a lot of bad things. But now, it's like I just sit and think about the choices I have to make between me going to school and me hanging out with my cousins. It's like I really didn't used to care about school but now I think about it like I'm going to have to be something in order to succeed in life.

Another male student commented, "The program provides a purpose for me. Most people just go through and just try to get through. It kind of shines the light at the end of the tunnel with college." As mentioned by both of these students, trying to "get through" school was a common sentiment felt by the students prior to obtaining college knowledge. With the opportunities provided by the program as well as the continual push from the program staff toward college attainment, the students' ideas about their academic capabilities and postsecondary pursuits changed.

Because the Compact Scholarship is an integral part of the program—and the students' long-range goal in the program—many of these students are motivated to do well. One student from Boys to Men expressed this motivation clearly: "[The director] said if you do good on your ACT and stay in high school and keep up your grades . . . he said you can get a four-year scholarship, and that's what made me want to do well." Another student from Boys to Men thought of the scholarship as the ultimate reward of being a part of the program: "The best prize we get when we graduate from high school is scholarships. . . . You need good grades and we ain't got to pay for college."

As discussed by the students and program staff, college knowledge is a critical piece of the mentorship program. Students not only work hard to do well in school but also strive to achieve the Compact Scholarship so they will be financially secure during college.

Mentorship
Mentorship is one of the key components of the program. For the Center for Student Advocacy, the mentorship consists of two components: peer mentorship and staff mentorship. Peer mentorship includes group check-ins, idea-sharing, and general social interaction among the students. Staff mentorship includes individual check-ins regarding academic planning and behavioral management. Both types of mentorship work in conjunction with one another to provide effective learning and positive student outcomes.

Peer mentorship is a strong driving force for positive peer influence and student retention in the program. The students described their relationship with one another as something similar to that of a family. One male student said,

> With the few of us, we built a brotherhood. If I see [my peer] not doing something right . . . with all of us in the same group I feel comfortable telling him that's wrong. [The director] doesn't want you doing that. We have each other's backs as Boys to Men.

A female student also felt that way: "You know we're family; we may not get along but we're all family. We're just a dysfunctional family but we're all going to make it one day." Both groups of students emphasized family, specifically the brother- and sisterhood, as an important part of their peer mentorship experience. This familial relationship provides a space for students to motivate one another and build a commitment to grow together.

As brothers and sisters who are a part of a larger family, the students developed codependent relationships with one another; they not only go to each other for help but also keep each other accountable. One male student spoke of this positive influence and peer accountability:

> Amazingly enough, we're all peers and we are able to influence each other more than [the director] or somebody. Even the senior mentors, they are able to relate to us like how we feel and what we think about things. You know if somebody got some stupid idea, we're able to influence them to do something better. Or even if they just need somebody to back them up, we're able to do something like that because you know we are all trying to get to the same place—get out of Detroit hopefully.

Another male student reiterated the positive impact of peer mentorship:

> We relate to each other. We talk about problems and try to solve them. We try to help each other reach our goals and we learn from each other. We do things as a team; we work together as a team and be leaders and not followers.

A female student shared a similar sentiment:

> It's like the realest [sic] group you can come to. . . . If you do something wrong or if you're going through something we're straightforward. Sometimes it is tough love but it's love at the same time. . . . We're all like sisters and so any of us doing wrong we're going to tell you.

Keeping each other accountable and working together as a team were commonly identified as crucial components of the students' academic development, which allowed the students to influence each other in positive ways. Several students spoke of peer mentorship as not only a vehicle for peer motivation but also a space for group validation and uplift. As articulated by a male student,

> You see things around you and you know you want to motivate yourself and motivate others to not become a statistic. You see all of us here are young Black males and I'm not going to say everybody but a lot of

people might not want to see us succeed so that's what keeps me going. People say I can't do stuff; you know, that draws me, makes me persevere.

Ultimately, the mentorship program focuses on the development of the whole student, emphasizing academics, navigational skills, interpersonal skills, leadership, and building knowledge about college. Most importantly, the mentorship component is tailored to the learning needs of each individual student, to enable him or her to become a well-rounded individual.

Community Exposure
A unique part of the program is that the students are provided with the opportunity to be exposed to environments outside the context of their school and, most noteworthy, Detroit. The program curriculum includes monthly field trips, cultural events, and bringing different community members into the school for workshops and inspiring conversations. One male student spoke about this unique component: "It takes us out of the city and gives us different experiences, like going to college or going out to Ypsilanti, Michigan, just to see what things are like outside of Detroit." While having a supportive network at school is important, the emphasis on exposure outside Detroit is very valuable to the students as it offers them opportunities to expand their viewpoints.

The purpose of the monthly field trips goes beyond simply taking the students out of the city; the staff ensures that the students get meaningful experiences and lessons out of the trips. A female student talked about a specific field trip they participated in that inspired her tremendously:

> Not last year but the first year we actually had the opportunity to go to Chicago to see Judge Mathis. We, like, toured around and then later Judge Mathis actually came down here. When he was speaking, he was telling us about how at first he was a troubled kid and then he had mentors help him along and it inspired him. I know it inspired me to get my attitude together and to start actually doing work. At first I didn't really care about school and now I do.

Seeing Judge Mathis and hearing him speak about his troubled past inspired the student to work on her behavior and academics; she was able to relate to him since she had been a troubled youth herself. Several students expressed the notion of "making it out." One male student spoke of this newfound goal: "I see within the program, a lot of us are really trying to make their lives better and all persevere. We all really just are striving for one thing and that's to make it out." Through the exposure to different environments and positive adult figures outside Detroit, the students are motivated to do well in their academics and instilled with a greater purpose of "making it out"—whether to make it out of their immediate city, their current circumstances, or their school (i.e., graduate)—the students are empowered by these exposures to strive to become their best selves. With the support of and opportunities offered by the program, these students are able to think of themselves as strivers, leaders, and individuals who will be successful in beating the statistics.

Program Challenges

As a comprehensive mentoring program in its pilot stage, the Center for Student Advocacy has provided a valuable and positive experience for all participants. Over the three-year time frame, the students in the program have improved their grades and some have excelled in school (e.g., a student became valedictorian). Moreover, the students have improved their behavior and developed goals toward college attainment. In spite of these successes, many of the students and program staff expressed concerns regarding the sustainability of the program.

Financial support remained a challenge. The program continues to face a lack of funding, which affects the hiring of staff, additional programming for the students, and outreach. Although the program received several in-kind donations for its activities, the lack of financial assurance from external funders proved to be stressful for the staff of the program. A staff member from Boys to Men spoke clearly about this challenge: "We need to provide the director with an additional support because he is divided between here and Ladies of Distinction. So, if we could get another person that is as committed as he, we can maybe even add more students." Another staff member from Boys to Men spoke similarly: "The director can't do everything. We need more people to step in and help him run the program. Because the program is growing, and with growth you try to add new programs and new developments and new people." At the current level of development, staff members are very limited and most of them are volunteers. Furthermore, the director works with both schools, which limits his time to work with the students.

The lack of funding also adversely affects programming for the students. One staff member of Ladies of Distinction articulated this directly:

> Money. Field trips cost money. A lot of times I've gotten free field trips but buses cost money; everything costs money. . . . I'm looking for a partner who can do a two- or three-year stint so that we can be assured that we'll have the things that we know are proven to be successful, and field trips are one of them.

A male student spoke of wishing for more services from the program:

> A friend told us a while ago they have this program at Michigan where it was over the summer. Nothing like an internship but just like . . . he was able to get what college life is about. He was able to live on campus. I would like to get something like that . . . more things outside of the school.

Now going into their fourth year in the program, students have transitioned out of middle school and into high school. As a result of this transition, many of the students are showing interest in getting college experiences; in order to meet the students' new needs, the program will require more funding. Many wish the program could be expanded to reach more students, considering the positive impact it has clearly had, but lack of funding has made this impossible.

Program Improvement

In order to be competitive in receiving external funding to address the challenges expressed by the students and staff (e.g., more staff, additional programming, outreach), student outcome data need to be collected and strengthened. This includes both qualitative and quantitative data collection. Finding a group of students with similar demographics to use as a control group for comparison is also recommended.

Creating partnerships with other middle and high schools is a critical step toward bringing this intervention to scale. The program should conduct meetings with various school leaders to discuss strategies to expand this pilot program into other schools.

Uses of the Research

Wesley Ganson

I am thrilled to extend my sincere gratitude for all of the research the research team provided to the Center for Student Advocacy. As I look back on the past year, I am reminded of your vital assistance to our program. Without your research, I would not have been able to seek the needed funding or feedback to refine and expand a higher-quality, comprehensive mentoring program to the students at Frederick Douglass and Detroit International Academies. Here are a few examples:

1. The research has refined the program through the feedback of the students at both schools who were interviewed by your staff.
2. The research has given potential funders valuable information about the positive impact the program has had on student participants at Fredrick Douglass and Detroit International Academies.

Additionally, the research has given me and my volunteer staff essential information to gain the necessary funding and the feedback from student participants to make the necessary program adjustments so that the program can be expanded to impact more students and schools within the DPS and other districts.

Reflective Questions

The Editors

1. How does this research inform collective understanding of college preparation during high school?
2. How does this research relate to scholarship on high school mentoring and teaching?
3. What are the benefits to graduate student researchers of engaging in research partnerships with community-based advocates?
4. How does community-based research broaden the training of graduate students interested in higher and urban education?

> 5. Are there programs in your context that have never or rarely been evaluated?
> 6. What aspects of the needs and programming in the Center for Student Advocacy are similar to and different from your context?
> 7. How do mentoring and encouragement help inform students about potential college pathways?
> 8. How do the patterns of student engagement compare to the survey results in the CFES case?
> 9. How might interviews help your organization learn about and advocate for students?

Case 4.4

Teacher Interviews: Integrating Advanced Math Courses Into Urban Schools

Max Altman and Jerry L. Rankin

Michigan now requires students to take Algebra II for high school graduation. To ensure all students have the opportunity to graduate, it is essential that urban middle and high schools transform math education. It is not just a matter of implementing a new curriculum; it is also essential to transform pedagogy to engage students who are not predisposed toward abstract math. This case focuses on professional development for teachers in an urban independent high school facing this new challenge. It also illustrates the deep structural and social issues confronted by educators and interventionists involved in integrating advanced math into inner-city high schools. This case has three parts:

1. Jerry L. Rankin describes the professional development support he provided.
2. Max Altman reports findings based on interviews with teachers who participated in professional development provided by Rankin.
3. Rankin follows up after Altman's report.

Professional Development at Detroit Technology Academy

Jerry L. Rankin

I developed a model called the Coordinate Geometry Project (CGP) to provide professional development (PD) to teachers to help them teach advanced math; I field-tested this model at the Detroit Technology Academy (DTA). CGP is a module presented to boost students' self-validation by creating layers of illustrations for similar applications with different formulas. The project builds on students' need to feel smart by managing similar processes with formulas that include signed numbers.

The pedagogy for the PD was designed to help teachers engage students to *make sense* of mathematics for the most challenging category of the ACT by reinforcing a familiar reference to basic operations. Students' responses build momentum for learning and confirm their potential for solving coordinate geometry problems on the Michigan Merit Exam and the ACT. The benefit from the CGP is that it enables students to proceed with more or less complex formulas to reinforce problem-solving with real-world applications.

The first PD for most teachers interviewed lasted about four hours and featured ways of creating illustrations to enhance *sense making* with several layers of similar formulas for linear equations. A second PD models a classroom presentation for teachers to observe their students overcoming barriers to understanding *signed numbers* with formulas that require multiple steps for processing algebraic expressions. This benefits students' ability to proceed through the gateway to progressive math studies by processing all levels of algebraic expressions.

The PD is supported with one or two days of on-site modeling, with lessons that allow students to demonstrate sense making and willingness to become self-directed problem solvers. As they participate in breaking down complex formulas with their knowledge of basic operations, they demonstrate capacity for continued growth.

The momentum from creating the CGP enables continued sense making for progressive studies by demonstrating its relevance for learning. *Reasoning* and *problem-solving* build experiences and momentum for ACT problem-solving with categories: plane geometry, pre-algebra, elementary algebra, and intermediate algebra problems; trigonometry problems (developed with The Linus Project); and plane geometry and trigonometry.

Teachers were provided DVDs with an animated presentation of *The Coordinate Geometry Project* and *The Coordinate Geometry GPA Math Challenge (Jeopardy Game)* (e.g., Rankin, 2014) to assess students' proficiency for problem-solving with a range of simple to complex problems similar to ones students would encounter on the ACT. Students' demonstration of proficiency is reinforced with an assignment for them to create their version of the most complex problems; these problems will, in turn, reinforce and challenge the problem-solving skills of peers.

Analysis of Interview With Teachers

Max Altman

This study sought to discover how teachers who attended Jerry L. Rankin's workshops viewed challenges in teaching advanced math. To investigate the ways teachers understand their own contexts and in turn better inform teacher PD, I conducted interviews with two teachers at DTA and two teachers at another high school. Due to the extremely small sample size, none of the information presented is intended to generalize to all teachers, although I do at times speculate about possible patterns and whether they might hint at something more general. I asked the teachers a series of questions about the relationships they saw among their local context and their school, their students and students' families, their teaching beliefs, and their actual teaching actions, as well as one question about equity/social justice and how they understood the concept(s). Using the interview transcripts, I analyzed teachers' comments to explore the ways they see relationships among contextual factors and what that means in general, as well as for professional development in particular. The following analyzes interviews conducted in support of the professional development program.

The interviews were coded for strings of meaning described by teachers. First, all teacher comments that described a contextual factor or issue were noted. These comments were examined to determine, in addition to the issue discussed, what the teachers indicated as the source and the target of the issue, as well as whether the issue was presented as positive, negative, or neutral.

For example, in the teacher comment "I know that the parents that come up and check on their students, the students tend to respond to that, if a parent is up here or they know that their parent will come up, even the thought of us calling," the issue mentioned is school visits (which are framed as a positive thing), and the stated source of the issue is families.[2] For the purpose of my analysis, a *source* refers to the person, group, or institution that causes an issue to arise.

A *target* is the person, group, or institution impacted by an issue, based on the teacher's analysis rather than my own. In the foregoing example regarding parental presence in the school, the target is students because the teacher indicates that students respond to parent visits. This is again quite different than if she had said, for example, that a knowledge of the possibility of parent visits makes the classroom a more comfortable place (in which case the target would have been the classroom) or that parents who visit make the teacher's job easier (in which case the target would have been the teacher). Teachers identified a fairly small number of sources and targets, and the vast majority of issues were attributed to one of only three or four commonly mentioned people or groups (Table 4.13).

TABLE 4.13
Items Cited by Teachers as Sources and Targets of Issues

Source	Responses (n)	Target	Responses (n)
School	22	School	15
Students	22	Students	63
Families	26	Families	4
Classroom	0	Classroom	3
Teachers*	5	Teachers	3
Teacher	13	Teacher	11
Other^	37	Other+	26
Total (N)	125	Total (N)	125

*Referred to themselves: For example, if they made a comment such as "student behavior makes my job harder."
^Other things listed as sources of issues included the city (2 mentions), social class (2 mentions), administration (2 mentions), the private sector (2 mentions), the teacher's own high school (1 mention), the teacher's own teachers (1 mention), the teacher's mother (2 mentions), school staff (2 mentions), and the neighborhood (3 mentions), as well as 20 instances in which the source of an issue was unclear from a teacher's comment.
+Other things listed as targets of issues included Black students, suburban schools, urban schools, student aspirations, the district, the city (2 mentions), "people," the public schools, and socioeconomic problems (2 mentions), as well as 10 instances in which the target of an issue was unclear from a teacher's comment.

The interviews were coded, and the codes were examined for patterns and as departures from those patterns; codes were organized in several different ways in order to see those patterns. Issues mentioned by teachers multiple times were considered separately each time they were mentioned, although instances of identical issue, source, and target references were grouped (but still coded as having been mentioned more than once).

Analysis of Interviews
First, students are by far the most mentioned group, especially as targets, where they make up more than half of all mentions (Table 4.13). This is nearly three times as many instances as those in which they are cited as sources. Thus, it seems that, at least for these four teachers, students are the main outcome variable for the issues they discuss. The issues are varied, as are their sources, but the analysis of them as impacting students is consistent.

Second, the classroom is never mentioned as a source and mentioned only three times as a target. In total, it is mentioned less than the city and the same number of times as the neighborhood (which are included in the category of "other").[3] This could perhaps be because, although there were questions about the classroom in the interview, teachers responded to those questions by speaking about themselves or about students rather than by discussing the classroom specifically. The *classroom* is the only term on the list that does not refer to a concrete thing, since one can see the school, students, families, and teachers, and there is little debate on what those things mean. In contrast, classroom is an ambiguous construct, as it refers not to the physical classroom space but instead to teachers, students, and their interactions. Thus, discussing factors with teachers in terms of a classroom may not be the best way to communicate.

Third, and perhaps most interestingly, students' families were the most common source given by teachers but appear only four times as a target (and all four of these comments are from the same teacher, meaning that three out of four teachers did not list families as the target of a single issue). This illustrates a very important quality in the way these teachers think. While it is clear that families are impacted by many issues, the teachers interviewed saw them as being only the source of issues. This may be a contributor to the historical difficulty teachers and families often have in communicating productively. Viewing families as responsible for many student issues, even some that may not normally be thought of as being caused by families, such as attendance and charter school expansion, may cause a disconnect between teacher expectations and a family's actual ability to change circumstances. It would not be entirely unsupportable to claim that the two most important groups in students' lives, and the two most able to have positive impact under negative circumstances, are their families and their teachers. While these two groups can work wonders together, misunderstandings and miscommunications can put them at odds despite the fact they share the same goal—the education of children. It is important to think deeply about how teachers and families can each better appreciate the contextual situation of the other. Understanding more widely how teachers see students' families can be helpful to both groups in encouraging understanding and collaboration.

A few additional points of analysis related to the interviews are also worth considering here. First, there were no instances in which teachers described an issue that had its target as the school and its source as teacher(s). This does not necessarily indicate that teachers do not see themselves as capable of influencing the school, but not one teacher mentioned an instance in which he or she or a colleague currently does so. This is an interesting finding, as it is relatively common, in my own experience, to pitch ideas to teachers by telling them the new practice will improve the school. This may contrast with teachers' own ideas about their influence and its extent. Second, all but one of the mentions of the school as a target were negative, and all but five of the mentions of the school as a source were negative, which suggests that these teachers see the school as struggling against rather than benefiting from its local context, and that they also, on the whole, see it as constraining them and their students. Even though the teachers listed a series of positive qualities for the school (10 out of 17 qualities given were positive), these qualities were spoken of only generally and not as impacting anything.

Third, all but one of the strings citing students as a source were presented in a negative way. Teachers talked most about students, but they appeared to view most of what students contribute as negative. While a reconceptualization of students as positive contributors would clearly be a preferred change, such change would likely be very difficult to effect in a large-scale way. An explicit focus on the issues teachers cited and ways in which teachers can positively contribute to students in order to remedy what they see as negative issues may be a useful tactic when trying to ameliorate this negative construction of students.

Interpreting Findings
What does all of this mean? I would argue that these teachers have particular and relatively specific ways of talking about what is influenced and what does the influencing; in other words, the way one makes an argument to teachers for why the information in the PD is important might impact their ideas about its value. While this small sample is, of course, not representative, it does suggest that teachers perceive students as being influenced by many different factors. This is an important observation; one of the differences between the PD method used in this case and many others I have seen (as a high school math educator and graduate student) is that the presentation did not overemphasize test scores, school improvement, or social revolution. Instead, it was about students and the ways teachers can have a positive impact on student learning. Teachers appeared to conceptualize the PD in terms of student responses and student gains rather than broader or more general factors. Putting the focus on student improvement will likely continue to capture the attention of teachers in a way that general discussion cannot.

With this observation comes the added charge that teachers *are* seeing strings of meaning between the sources and targets of issues. Different teachers can see the same issue as impacting, or being impacted by, very different individuals or groups. For example, one teacher listed communication as a positive issue between administrators and teachers, and another teacher listed it as a negative issue between families and schools. Both to improve communication with teachers who are participating and enjoying the program and to perhaps better reach teachers who are not benefiting as much from it, it might be helpful to speak frankly with teachers about what they see as the sources and targets of the issues the PD aims to ameliorate. Talking to teachers about your own understanding of the sources and targets could be enlightening and may result in more buy-in, better participation, and more successful use of your ideas by teachers.

Finally, teachers may see additional issues beyond those commonly thought of as impacting urban schools. While there were certainly patterns in teacher responses, this small sampling of four teachers returned a striking 82 different issues among them. Regardless of whether all of these issues match with the factors others see, they represent ways teachers make meaning of their circumstances and should be respected as such. Asking teachers to identify what they see as important issues affecting their students (directly or indirectly) and their students' learning of math can inform your own approach to the discussion of the material. Thinking about possible ways to incorporate teacher ideas can make a strong presentation even stronger and more urgent. While my analysis of these data supports the moves I observed Rankin making in his professional development session, the only result of making a strong program stronger is greater success. An understanding of the many issues teachers see as salient and how they see the relationship between the sources and targets of these issues can make teachers into strong partners.

Reflections on Practice

Jerry L. Rankin

After receiving Altman's analysis, I modeled parts of the PD in classrooms for teachers' benefit at DTA and the Urban Middle School (UMS). The group of male students I worked with during sixth period at UMS demonstrated a strong performance on the Northwest Evaluation Association (NWEA) test and modeled the skills and willingness that will help teachers shift their paradigm. Teachers at UMS are now asking the right questions in preparation for their PD, which will encourage more eighth- and ninth-grade students to experience the benefits of problem-solving.

My goal is to create a contagious environment that impacts more students to anticipate proficiency based on increasing their willingness to participate in solving complex real-world problems with formulas that contain signed numbers. Students' success with this level of thinking prepares them to reinforce prerequisite skills more than traditional efforts to learn and build preparation for rigorous course work in earlier grades. The support and feedback from math teachers communicated by Altman's study are truly appreciated and invaluable in targeting needs and refining strategies for this endeavor.

Mathematics is a series of logical procedures. A student-focused perspective helps students build their expectations for success, addressing anticipated difficulties for underrepresented students that have limited their desire to pursue continued studies with career goals in STEM fields. Following are some specific considerations for success:

- Teachers need to address the impact of poor attendance on academic achievement for underrepresented students. Lack of attendance builds a significant barrier to students' immediate growth and reduces commitment to long-term achievement.
- Students' frequent failure to submit timely completed assignments is often a symptom of disinterest or withdrawal, or their way of avoiding identification with low achievement and potential failure to protect their self-image.
- Students identify with peers. The value of peer influence among underrepresented students provides a means of reshaping the cultural influences on low-income students.
- Students want to feel smart and challenged; they value their capacity to achieve challenging academic standards. A student-focused perspective enables students to make connections to build on their innate needs.

Mathematics is an exact science. Patterns that relate to prior experiences build on students' prior knowledge, which enables connections to familiar references to remediate required skills as needed and provides a way for them to reinforce relevance. Mathematical problem-solving challenges students to *make sense* of problems before they can solve them.

Instruction for today's underrepresented students should focus on presenting simple to complex problems for ongoing analysis, which challenges and enables student to relate their background knowledge to problem-solving. Underrepresented students enjoy the challenge of solving practice problems for the Common Core State Standards (CCSS) and ACT to validate and reinforce their untapped capacity for reasoning.

> **Reflective Questions**
>
> The Editors
>
> 1. How does the partnership between a graduate student researcher and a community math educator benefit the learning objectives of two partners?
> 2. What are the benefits of this partnership for Detroit students?
> 3. What does this case reveal about the complexity of math reform in urban high schools?
> 4. Understanding teachers' meaning-making in this case aided the practitioner in providing more relevant professional development. What would be gained by understanding staff beliefs and meaning-making in your context?
> 5. How might graduate programs in education organize to provide research support for the schools in their locales?
> 6. How should the voices of educators be considered in the design of interventions to implement new policies?
> 7. How did teachers' perceptions of students relate to the challenges they faced when teaching new, advanced subject matter?
> 8. How well did the interventionist reflect on the challenges raised by teachers when he refined his methods?
> 9. How might this iterative process of qualitative research and reflection be used to enhance implementation of new policies in K–12 and higher education, as well as the design of interventions and implementation of new polices?

Notes

1. DC is divided into eight wards with very distinctive racial, ethnic, and economic characteristics. We provided OSSE with detailed information on student success by ward in the full report.

2. Although teachers almost exclusively refer to *parents*, I use the word *families* in recognition of the fact that many students do not live with both parents and that parent roles are often assumed by people other than the student's biological parents. All teacher responses which referenced parents were coded as families, and no distinction was drawn in the ways in which teachers referred to families.

3. I have chosen to keep the classroom as a separate item on the list because several questions directly asked about it.

5

LEARNING FROM EXPERIENCE

Guidance 5: Learning From Experience

1. *Action inquiry builds organizational capacity breakdown barriers to change:* Public accountability systems generate data that can be used to support change agents who break down barriers to justice in education and other human systems.
2. *Practitioners build facilitative skills through reflection on experiences with engaged scholarship:* Practitioners share lessons they've learned from facilitating action inquiry.
3. *Engaged scholarship can be integrated across career pathways:* As a conclusion, a leading scholar reflects on mentoring practitioners and researchers interested in engaged scholarship promoting action inquiry.

It can be difficult for advocates to promote social justice within educational systems that emphasize public accountability and market mechanisms. The formal information systems capture data on students, but the data are seldom used to their benefit. The cases illustrate some of the ways political behavior undermines constructive use of data, but they also demonstrate that this system can be changed when new partnerships are constructed. The cases also document some of the ways data can be used. We share here the following reflections on engagement in the research-informed advocacy for educational and social justices:

- Kim Callahan Lijana reflects on her work as a change agent in high schools, along with her efforts as a graduate student to organize partnerships that use research to promote social justice in urban education systems.
- Glenda D. Musoba reflects on the process of working on engaged research projects in colleges and universities.
- Ed St. John reflects on the role of engaged scholarship in professional development of practitioners and professors.

Reflections on Action Inquiry in the Urban K–12 Context

Kim Callahan Lijana

Working in an urban school or district is difficult, but building robust partnerships with researchers and/or community organizations can be extremely rewarding for all involved. Collaboration between researchers and practitioners makes it easier to highlight the unique needs and strengths of the local student population and the various community stakeholders. The best partnerships provide all partners with new insights and an outside perspective as part of their collaboration on challenges important to both parties. However, getting the work up and running often involves complex negotiations and starts and stops. Action researchers need to be flexible and accommodating, understanding the complex roles and demands placed on school and district leaders.

Trust is essential in building a productive partnership. School and district leaders may have had negative experiences working with researchers in the past. Many urban communities and schools have been the experimentation ground for local universities, but they have gotten little that's meaningful in return; researchers need to focus on critical issues raised by the school and adding value to the community.

Trust in partnerships is about both the individual's character and the work. While I was working in a public charter high school as a college counselor, a researcher collected qualitative data about a college access program in the building. I left the interview feeling as though the questions asked were designed to validate the program and the researcher's preconceived beliefs. During the interview, I did not have the opportunity to share my perspective about what appeared to be missed opportunities and some of the challenges facing the student participants. Openness fosters trust and is essential in a research partnership; this experience did not allow me to be open.

A trusting partnership is built by listening more than speaking. It is extremely important to ask the right questions, carefully listen to the answers, and be open to new ideas when meeting with potential or current partners. What do they identify as critical issues? What do they value? Who are the key players? Determine if this is an area of mutual interest that can provide an opportunity for you to add value by collaborating on a meaningful project.

Unless you have a prior relationship with a key player in the school or district, persistence and patience are prerequisites to establishing a strong research partnership. In practice, this means finding opportunities to meet potential partners at conferences, community events, and other occasions that bring educators together. Do not underestimate the value of your professional network. Always take the opportunity to talk with someone to learn more about potential shared interests. Consistent, ongoing communication over e-mail, on the phone, and in person is necessary to get the research partnership off the ground and overcome typical challenges.

Urban education communities can be small; you never know where a new contact may take you. It is not uncommon for new contacts to suggest a few people they want to e-connect you with or to encourage you to send an introductory note to a few of their colleagues. Follow-up is extremely important. As a partner, you need to be proactive and reliable, making communication and follow-up easy. Urban education communities can also be in states of flux, which may mean you lay the groundwork for a partnership and find that a key supporter has moved on to another position; however, since people often move on, their networks can be large, and they may want to involve you in their new opportunity.

Being flexible and open provides endless possibilities. As you establish a reputation within the community, people will start seeking out your expertise. It is important to determine which organizations and schools are ready for a partnership with you and your organization and when you should direct them to other individuals and organizations that may be a better fit. Determining criteria for partnership can help guide this process, building on strong, open relationships. Collaboration between researchers and educators makes it possible to highlight the unique needs and strengths of the local student population and the various community stakeholders. This provides a tremendous opportunity to take advantage of locally available skills and resources. When researchers understand the local context and the strength of their partner(s), it is possible to build on the existing foundation and determine key areas for intervention and capacity building that leverage the strengths of the stakeholders and fill gaps when necessary.

In my experience working with schools and districts, there are several consistent challenges in building a mutually beneficial research partnership. In all cases, building and leveraging strong relationships are the key to moving the work forward. Making progress helps build momentum and often increases partnership buy-in. Following are a few of those important challenge areas:

- *Finalizing a memo of understanding.* A memo of understanding is a requirement to conduct research in most schools and districts. In charter and independent schools, the process of gaining access is typically easier and may require only the approval of the principal or a school leader. In public and large urban districts, approval typically requires signatures of school leadership, the superintendent of the district, and the school board. As soon as the partnership and project are in the planning phases, it is critical to work with key personnel to develop and finalize a memo of understanding.
- *Obtaining quantitative data from the district.* Even after the memo of understanding is signed, the district and research office have to provide access and share the district's data; in the Detroit case, this took over a year. Developing relationships across the district offices can be extremely important. Key personnel can assist when there are problems in the process.
- *Working with district-level personnel.* You need to develop strong relationships with individuals at various levels in the district office. In order for the work to go smoothly, you need support from both the top of the district (i.e., superintendent) and from within the schools (i.e., principal or other school leader). In addition, it is essential to build strong relationships with the individuals responsible for the district's data systems. Receiving the data in a usable format results in more timely analysis.
- *Identifying and gaining access to schools.* Determining which specific schools to work with and then gaining access take local insight and on-the-ground expertise. Use extant data and collaborate with the working group and district to identify target schools. Ask the

working group to tap into their networks to start conversations about engaging in school-level work.
- *Working with school-level personnel to collect qualitative data.* At each school you need a point person who understands the project and can identify key individuals to interview. Setting up an interview schedule that is time-efficient, works within the school's structures, and captures the voices of all stakeholders relevant to the project requires in-depth understanding of the school and the help of an individual who has enough influence to persuade interview participants to prioritize this work.

In the following, I present a few recommendations for implementing the action inquiry model (AIM) in urban school district partnerships:

- *Collect and incorporate all stakeholders.* Provide the opportunity for everyone at the table to have a voice. Have a conversation identifying key stakeholders and individuals and organizations that are on the margins. Identifying a process to collect and incorporate all stakeholder voices is extremely important and a powerful outcome of implementing AIM.
- *Negotiate group dynamics.* Dynamics in the working group can be complicated, and action researchers need to be aware of the power of their voices at the table. Community and school partners may defer to university personnel and/or think that the partnership will lead to special relationships and preferential treatment for their students or funding of special projects. Understanding the power dynamics and being open and transparent provide the opportunity for more voices to be heard and empower practitioners to take a more active role in the work.
- *Have the "right" people at the table.* Work group members need to be respected and able to bring implementation recommendations to the individuals who can make things happen. It is not always clear at the start of the project who these people are. As the work progresses, you may realize that the group would benefit from adding a few key individuals. Be thoughtful about how to bring this up to the group and how to introduce and get new members up to speed.

- *Identify a critical issue worth addressing.* The work group needs to develop a shared mission and questions that are important to all partners. Identifying a critical issue that everyone wants to address is a great starting point. Developing the questions together leads to all partners being invested in the process and results. Setting up the work well will influence how the results are received and the likelihood they will be used to revise and refine programming.
- *Value continuous improvement.* Work group leaders need to be open to and value continuous improvement in the partnership and its projects. Both researchers and practitioners may have invested significant time and energy developing their programs and beliefs about potential solutions to critical challenges. Learning that their solution did not have the intended effect is often discouraging. Using the inquiry process to learn and more deeply understand the challenge will lead to new innovative solutions.
- *Define clear outcomes and intended audience.* The composition and goals of the work group will help determine the outcomes and audience. For example, in the Detroit case, the mission of the work group was clear but very broad—improved educational outcomes and opportunities for Detroit students. Work groups tackling significant long-term challenges will benefit from identifying short-term objectives.

Reflections on Engaged Research in Colleges and Universities

Glenda D. Musoba

Too often there is a gap between knowledge producers and knowledge users. This gap leaves the institutional research office producing reports that they wonder if anyone reads and administrators utilizing best practice from other institutions, professional instincts, or research conducted in another context. Administrators bemoan the lack of data, and the institutional research office is closer to the state data office than their colleagues on campus.

Collaborating through AIM to address critical issues can lead to a satisfying relationship between administrators and researchers because it bridges this divide. Administrators can ask real-time questions, which means institutional researchers know their efforts are likely to result in program improvements that directly benefit students; administrators get answers to their questions from their own student population. As a result, institutions can develop a culture where the first source of information is their own institutional data rather than best practice from other institutions, some very different from their own, with clear differences in context and types of students. This is particularly problematic when minority-serving institutions, community colleges, and commuter institutions copy best practices from predominantly White, upper-middle-class, residential institutions. Collaboration between researchers and practitioners who are part of the institution makes it easier to highlight the unique needs and strengths of the local student population.

I present here the following few guidelines:

- *Buy-in from senior leadership must be evident to the inquiry group.* Making this collaboration work can initially be time-consuming and challenging. Those who are involved need to know that central administration will support recommended changes that result from their efforts. Senior leadership does not necessarily need to participate in the day-to-day workings of the inquiry group, but the group must feel their support and interest; participants need to know they are connected to powerful people within the university who can facilitate change. For example, a student services director showed little interest in the research findings regarding her area until she saw that the central administration was paying attention to the research groups' findings.
- *Midlevel administrators who direct or coordinate the programs are ideal practitioners for the work group.* Work group members must be senior enough to have the power to make change, but junior enough that the recommendations for change will be coming from within the units. Ideally, program directors will be those who can quickly make changes to their practice as a result of the research evidence. Multiple times we observed quick changes from administrators once the research pointed to an improvement that could be made in their office. We also observed frustrated entry-level professionals trying to make change without influence.
- *Practitioners who operate the programs must be involved in selecting the research questions.* Practitioners will have much more ownership

over the results of the study if they were involved in developing the questions asked. On several campuses where there was a change in program leadership from when the research questions were formulated to when the recommendations from the research were presented, the new leader showed little or no interest in the research. The new administrators had arrived with their own agenda, were brought in because they had expertise on the topic, and found it difficult to take advice from a work group. In contrast, even when administrators did not like the findings, when they were involved in developing the research they owned the results and made adjustments.

- *An attitude of pilot testing and constant revision is important.* Sometimes, practitioners are so confident the new program will work that they are committed to it before the research results are presented; if the results show the program they advocate is not working, they can resist revision. When practitioners have invested substantial energy and time in developing a new program, it can be difficult to hear it does not solve the problem. When practitioners see their own practice as research, they are more open to the results and further revision. This is important because multiple cycles through the inquiry process may be required, and multiple programs that each address a part of the problem may need to be developed.
- *A shift in culture is needed that considers negative results as helpful for learning rather than having negative consequences.* Inquiry for critical issues must be decoupled from employee performance evaluation and job insecurity. If people are worried about their jobs, they can resist research in order to protect their role; when they are confident their position is secure and that the research will help them learn how to do a better job serving students, they can be invested in the project. It may be considered safer for job security to just copy a successful university rather than try something totally new, but the totally new program may be what is needed to address a critical issue.
- *The majority of the work group has to identify the critical issue as something they want to address.* Ideally, the work group selects the issue or members choose a work group based on their concerns about the issue, rather than receiving a topic assigned from above. If group members are to be committed and faithfully attend the

work group, taking time from busy schedules to work on these issues, they need to believe that what they are doing has value.

Reflections on Engaged Scholarship Across Career Pathways

Ed St. John

- *Engaged scholarship helps us make reflective turns within our career pathways.* After studying action science and theories of systemic change in graduate school, as an early career professional, I frequently reflected on the social consequences of my work as an analyst in state and federal agencies and as a manager in the consulting industry. In 1989, I decided to become an academic, working with partners to promote social justice within the emerging market systems developing in education. Since that time I've learned that people take a reflective turn at many points within their career pathways. For example, many early career professionals choose to pursue advanced graduate degrees after reflecting on their early professional experiences. For additional perspectives of reflection in action see Donald Schön's (1987, 1991) groundbreaking books *Educating the Reflective Practitioner: Toward a New Design for Teaching and Learning In the Professions* and *The Reflective Turn: Case Studies In and On Educational Practice*.
- *Emerging scholars benefit from mentoring that encourages engaged scholarship.* For nearly three decades, I've worked with graduate students interested in integrating their research into initiatives supporting social justice in education. As a result I've also collaborated with graduate students on books about family engagement in schools (e.g., St. John, Griffith, & Allen-Haynes, 1997); early reading reform (e.g., St. John, Loescher & Bardzell, 2003); and college preparation, access, and success (various references cited in this volume). As Lijana's and Musoba's reflections earlier in this chapter illustrate, this process often continues after graduate school. Since their graduation, I've continued to work with them on academic projects growing out of scholarship to support social justice initiatives (e.g., St. John, Bigelow, Lijana, & Masse, 2015; St. John & Musoba, 2010).
- *Practitioners can refine their practices by working with engaged scholars.* The cases in this guidebook were written by researchers

in collaboration with practitioners. They illustrate some of the ways practitioners learn from collaborating with emerging scholars. Partnerships can generate new forms of knowledge for action. For example, based on the projects described in the cases, Rick Dalton took leadership on writing *College for Every Student: A Practitioner's Guide to Building College and Career Readiness* (Dalton & St. John, 2016), a book written for educators and social activists interested in developing local initiatives that support college and career preparation for students from low-income neighborhoods and schools.

AFTERWORD

Using Action Inquiry in Engaged Research: An Organizing Guide is quintessential Ed St. John. What makes this guide so valuable is that it weaves together St. John's passion (as well as the passion of Kim Callahan Lijana, Glenda D. Musoba, and the other contributors) for research and social justice. Using action inquiry can rebuild the relationship between research and educational and, ultimately, social and economic equality.

Engaged research is a viable and sound strategy for solving the rampant inequality in the United States. The organization I lead, College For Every Student (CFES), is founded on the beliefs that educational inequality affects economic opportunity and that it is far and away our greatest domestic challenge. When you consider that the United States has a greater wealth gap by race than South Africa did during apartheid, you realize that we desperately need strategies that work.

The solution is education, specifically a college degree. A college degree is today's finish line. It's the equivalent of a high school diploma a generation ago, and young people denied college will be without high-paying jobs in our new economy.

The ideas, inspirations, and practical steps in *Using Action Inquiry in Engaged Research* provide a strategic blueprint for reducing inequality within the systems we now have in education.

The need for this book has never been greater. *Using Action Inquiry in Engaged Research* references "the growing income inequality in the United States that provides a complicated and troubling context for education reforms" (p. 6). In fact, the inequality gap in every educational measure (e.g., high school graduation, college-going, college completion, standardized test scores) between low-income students and their higher-income peers has widened every year since 1980. When you consider that the fastest-growing cohort of youth in the United States is defined by poverty, you soon realize that we stand at the edge of the precipice.

All of this is happening at a time when the United States and other nations need educated citizens more than ever to meet economic, social, and democratic challenges. In the next 10 years, the United States will be unable to fill 23 million jobs because we won't have enough educated/skilled workers. At the same time there will be more than 25 million young citizens unemployed or underemployed, not because they lack ability, but because they were denied the opportunity for postsecondary training and schooling simply because they grew up in low-income households.

To combat this disastrous trend, St. John and colleagues advocate that we, as practitioners, "develop a preliminary actionable theory" (p. 1, this volume), and that we continually refine our theory and action plan through research, partners, and other action research steps. CFES is founded on the immutable belief that we need to increase the number of low-income children who attain college degrees. All of our theories and strategies emanate from this core belief.

Our action research has led us to the conclusion that underserved youth have rudimentary needs that must be addressed to ensure they move toward college-success readiness. The foundational need for low-income youth is hope: They must believe they can grasp the American dream and attend college. Once young people are given hope for a better future, they can then aspire to new possibilities: *I can attend a community college and become a nurse. I can graduate from a four-year university and become an engineer.* All along the way, we must help young people develop what we term the *essential skills*. These include adaptability, perseverance, grit, leadership, and other competencies.

CFES believes that academic rigor can be built on these competencies and skills, but the notion that tougher standards are the foundational answer is fallacy. In agreement with our theory, this guide states that "raising high school graduation requirements [to] equalize educational and economic opportunity for all students is a *deceptive myth*" (pp. 6–7, this volume). Federal educational policy has been obsessed with standardized tests for three decades and is inherently counterproductive in trying to achieve educational success for underrepresented populations. It's time for the new paradigm that *Using Action Inquiry in Engaged Research* advances.

CFES's theories have developed over two decades of using action inquiry as part of which we continually reevaluate our strategies and environment for improvement. Our journey has even involved a name change. The organization was called Foundation for Excellent Schools until 2006, when we spent an intensive eight months of testing our foundational theories, interventions, and even our messaging and nomenclature. We learned through focus groups and surveys (action inquiry) and with the aid of a national task force of college presidents, philanthropists, and K–12 and corporate leaders that our organizational name did not accurately describe our mission and values.

During this intensive and often uncomfortable introspective process, it became clear that we needed ongoing external support to accelerate and deepen our continuous improvement process. We compiled a list of individuals and organizations that might help us with research and evaluation. An intern who had just completed her master's in educational leadership suggested St. John, whom she dubbed "the rock star researcher on college access and social justice," and we reached out to him.

At CFES, we know we must constantly adapt our strategies and even the language that describes our approach, and we must provide local solutions. Our leadership through service and mentoring practices, for example, play out differently depending on the culture and location of a particular student population. Our external team from the University of Michigan helps us see the subtleties between and among our student populations in different locales: Dublin, Ireland; Harlem; a reservation in South Dakota; and the rural hills on the Big Island of Hawaii.

The cases in this volume illustrate how CFES built a partnership with St. John's research team. Evidence generated by St. John and his colleagues has helped us evolve our practices to address challenge in the communities we serve. As an outgrowth of this collaboration, St. John and I recently published the book, *College For Every Student: A Practitioner's Guide to Building College and Career Readiness* (Routledge, 2016).

Rick Dalton
President and Chief Executive Officer
College For Every Student

REFERENCES

Coleman, J. S. (1988). Social capital in the creation of human capital. *American Journal of Sociology, 94,* S95–S120.

Dalton, R., Bigelow, V., & St. John, E. P. (2012). College For Every Student: A model for postsecondary encouragement in rural schools. In R. Winkle-Wagner, P. J. Bowman, & E. P. St. John (Eds.), *Expanding postsecondary opportunity for underrepresented students: Theory and practice of academic capital formation. Readings on equal education* (Vol. 26, pp. 181–204). New York, NY: AMS Press.

Dalton, R., & St. John, E. P. (2016). *College For Every Student: A practitioner's guide to building college and career readiness.* New York, NY: Routledge/Eye on Education.

Holmes, D. R. (1986). *Frontiers of possibility: Report of the National College Counseling Project.* Burlington: University of Vermont.

Hossler, D., Ziskin, M., & Gross, J. (2009). Getting serious about institutional performance in students retention: Research-based lessons on effective policies and practice. *About Campus, 13*(6), 2–11.

Jones, R. (2004). *DC Tuition Assistance Grant Program annual report (2003–2004).* Washington, DC: Office of the State Superintendent of Education District of Columbia.

Kane, T. (2004). *Evaluating the impact of the D.C. Tuition Assistance Grant Program* (01/2004). Cambridge, MA: National Bureau of Economic Research Working Papers.

Lazere, E. (2007). *DC's two economies: Many residents are falling behind despite the city's revitalization.* Washington, DC: DC Fiscal Policy Institute.

Mattern, K. D., & Shaw, E. J. (2010). A look beyond cognitive predictors of academic success: Understanding the relationship between academic self-beliefs and outcomes. *Journal of College Student Development, 51*(6), 665.

Moore III, J. V., & Rago, M. A. (2009). Patterns in motivation and engagement among working students. In D. Hossler, J. Gross, & M. Ziskin (Eds.), *Enhancing institutional and state initiatives to increase student success: Studies of the Indiana Project on Academic Success. Readings on equal education* (Vol. 24, pp. 45–78). New York, NY: AMS Press.

Perna, L. W. (Ed.). (2012). *Preparing today's students for tomorrow's jobs in metropolitan America.* Philadelphia: University of Pennsylvania Press.

Rankin, J. L. (2014). *The coordinate geometry project student workbook*. Maitland, FL: Xulon Press, Inc.

Ravitch, D. (2010). *The death and life of the great American school system: How testing and choices are undermining education*. New York, NY: Basic Books.

Schön, D. A. (1987). *Educating the reflective practitioner: Toward a new design for teaching and learning in the professions*. San Francisco, CA: Jossey-Bass.

Schön, D. A. (Ed.). (1991). *The reflective turn: Case studies in and on educational practice*. New York, NY: Teachers College Press.

St. John, E. P. (2013). *Research, actionable knowledge and social change: Reclaiming social responsibility through research in partnerships with practitioners*. Sterling, VA: Stylus.

St. John, E. P., Griffith, A. I., & Allen-Haynes, L. (1997). *Families in schools: A chorus of voices in restructuring*. Portsmouth, NH: Heinemann.

St. John, E. P., Bigelow, V. M., Lijana, K., & Masse, J. (2015). *Left behind: Urban high schools and the failed market*. Baltimore, MD: Johns Hopkins University Press.

St. John, E. P., Hu, S., & Fisher, A. S. (2011). *Breaking through the access barrier: Academic capital formation informing public policy*. New York, NY: Routledge.

St. John, E. P., Loescher, S. A., & Bardzell, J. S. (2003). *Improving reading and literacy in grades 1–5: A resource guide to research-based programs*. Thousand Oaks, CA: Corwin.

St. John, E. P., & Musoba, G. D. (2010). *Pathways to academic success: Expanding opportunity for underrepresented students*. New York, NY: Routledge.

Winkle-Wagner, R., Bowman, P. J. & St John, E. P. (Eds). (2012). *Expanding postsecondary opportunity for underrepresented students: Theory and practice of academic capital formation. Readings on equal education*, (Vol. 26). New York, NY: AMS Press, Inc.

Ziskin, M., Torres, V., Hossler, D. & Gross, J. P. K. (2010). Mobile working students: A delicate balance of college, family, and work. In L. W. Perna (Ed.), *Understanding the working college student: New research and its implications for policy and practice*. Sterling, VA: Stylus.

ABOUT THE CONTRIBUTORS

Max Altman is a doctoral candidate at the University of Michigan and a former high school math teacher. His research interests lie in creating K–12 educational policy reflecting social justice initiatives and determining how the contexts in which teachers and students operate shape their conceptions of equity and social justice.

Victoria J. Milazzo Bigelow received her PhD from the University of Michigan Center for the Study of Higher and Postsecondary Education, where she is currently a postdoctoral research fellow. She is a former coordinator for advanced degree teacher certification and instructor of education and music at Marygrove College. She is a coauthor of *Left Behind: Urban High Schools and the Failure of Market Reform* (Johns Hopkins University Press, 2015) and several articles related to school-college partnerships, academic capital formation, and the transfer experience for minority STEM students.

Anna Chiang received her MA in higher education at the University of Michigan and her BA in ethnic studies at the University of California, Berkeley. Her academic interest is in higher education access and outcomes for underrepresented student populations. Currently, she is an academic adviser at Alliant International University, where she works with graduate students on their academic program planning. She also facilitates initiatives to ensure positive student learning experiences and outcomes.

Rick Dalton has worked for the past two decades to make College For Every Student (CFES) a global leader in helping underserved students gain access to college and be successful there. CFES has helped more than 75,000 students in 40 states to graduate from high school and attend college. His doctoral work at Harvard on the connection between organizational behavior and educational opportunity laid the foundation for

CFES. While director of enrollment planning at Middlebury College, he created a partnership with a high school in the Bronx that led to the creation of 120 school-college partnerships. He has written more than 130 articles and op-eds on educational issues.

Amy S. Fisher earned her PhD from the University of Michigan in 2013. Her research interests include financial aid policy; access, retention, and success of low-income students; and social justice. She is coauthor of *Breaking Through the Access Barrier: Academic Capital Formation Informing Public Policy* (Routledge, 2011).

Wesley Ganson is an educator in the Detroit Public Schools. He has earned a BA in political science, two MA degrees in communication and education, and an EdSp degree in educational leadership, all from Eastern Michigan University. He is currently pursuing a PhD in educational leadership from Wayne State University.

Leanne Kang is a recent PhD graduate in educational foundations and policy at the University of Michigan and a graduate research assistant for the Detroit Schools–Higher Education Consortium. Her dissertation examined school governance change over the last 30 years in Detroit.

Kim Callahan Lijana is a managing director of school support for The Achievement Network, a mission-driven education nonprofit. She recently completed a PhD at the University of Michigan Center for the Study of Higher and Postsecondary Education. Her research interests center on issues of educational equity with a focus on college preparation, college access, and college success for students who represent the first generation in their family to go to college. She is a coauthor of *Left Behind: Urban High Schools and the Failure of Market Reform* (Johns Hopkins University Press, 2015).

Rehva Jones McKinnon is currently director of data and evaluation with America Achieves' Teacher and Principal Fellowship Program. Passionate about the importance of equity in higher education, she continues to support first-generation college students as an adjunct faculty member in Washington, DC.

Glenda D. Musoba is an associate professor of higher education at Texas A&M University. Her research has focused on policies and practices that influence college student access and success, including financial aid and academic preparation. She is coauthor of *Pathways to Academic Success: Expanding Opportunity for Underrepresented Students* (Routledge, 2010). Most recently she has examined transfer student success and state transfer articulation policy.

Jerry L. Rankin has 30 years of experience addressing barriers to mathematical proficiency. He extends students' basic skills to decode math symbols to process advanced formulas. His hands-on projects align formulas to illustrations to build problem-solving skills at the level of Common Core State Standards and the ACT.

Edward P. St. John is Algo D. Henderson Collegiate Professor Emeritus at the University of Michigan's Center for the Study of Higher and Postsecondary Education. His scholarship focus is on education for a just society, an interest that stems from three decades of research on educational policy and practice. He is a Fellow of the American Educational Research Association and has received awards for leadership and research from the Association for the Study of Higher Education.

INDEX

academic achievement
  in old and new schools, 38–40
  opportunities actualized for, 11
  of students, 100–101
Academic Capital Formation (ACF), 55–56, 60–62
accountability
  adequacy of internal, 31–32
  in educational systems, 23
  mentoring programs teaching, 104–105
  surveys, research and, 98
  systems of, 31, 77–78
ACT, 38–39, 110
action. *See also* action inquiry
  design for plans of, 73
  guide for, 19–21, 42, 70
  information and analysis informing, 74
  reflection in, 127
actionable theory
  as adaptable, 7–8
  of change, 6–9, 47
  development of, 7–8, 10, 130
  identifying strategy for, 9
  intervention testing, 1
  partnerships assisted by, 11
  practice identifying strategy of, 9
  problems helped by, 47
  strategies for, 9
action inquiry
  barriers broken down by, 119
  cycle of, 5, 70–73

data analyzed by, 3
definition of, 5
engaged research, learning and, 69–70, 129
equity promoted by, 1
evaluation in cycle of, 46
inspiration for, 129
leadership in groups of, 125
model of, 123
partnerships built by, 48–49
research, social justice and, 48, 129
research and evaluation in, 73–74, 76
students empowered by, 6–7
in urban K-12 context, 120
use of, 41
advanced math, 109, 111, 117

barriers
  action inquiry breaking down, 119
  to college preparation, 15–16
  identifying of, 2, 18, 19, 21, 24, 25, 28
  reflection on, 14
  remedies organized for, 21–25
  research identifying, 71
  to social justice, 2, 18
  students facing, 19, 21, 22
  of underrepresented students, 22
  understanding of, 26
Bowman, Philip, 28

139

Boys to Men, 99–100, 103
Brown v. Board of Education, 27
Bush, George W., 52

case studies
    analyzing, 16
    learning from, 15–18
    for research change, 70–72
    research illustrated by, 15–16
    research strategies and, 42
CBOs. *See* community-based
    organizations
CFES. *See* College for Every
    Student
CGP. *See* Coordinate Geometry
    Project
challenges
    in community, 131
    as critical, 19, 37
    Detroit Consortium facing,
        66–68
    in education organizations,
        20–21
    identifying of, 4
    identifying of critical, 124,
        126–27
    intervention aligned with, 25
    in mentoring programs, 106–7
    in partnership building, 122
    for students, 97, 117
    teachers facing, 62–63
    underlying causes of, 24
    urban schools faced by, 26
change
    actionable theory of, 6–9, 47
    case studies for research, 70–72
    information used for, 2–3, 69
    intervention identified by, 7–8
    organizing for, 2, 41
    OSSE leadership, 53
    of policy as rapid, 13

    processes of, 5
    research making, 70, 125
    system support for, 47–48
    transfer or major, 20–21
the classroom, 113
Clinton, Bill, 52
Coleman, Mary Sue, 29
collaboration
    partnerships providing, 18, 120
    between researchers and teachers,
        121–22
    in schools and community, 46
College Explore, 58
College for Every Student (CFES),
    10, 15
    ACF and, 60–62
    capacity building in, 43
    core practices of, 30–31, 37, 58
    director support within, 57
    engaged research supporting, 60
    engagement in social support
        for, 94
    ethnicity of students of Green
        High School and, 92
    family engagement fostered by,
        30
    funding for, 29–30
    introduction to, 30–31
    leadership service offered by, 57
    local solutions provided by, 131
    mentoring relationships in, 56
    organization process of, 57
    partnerships of, 55, 56
    pilot study of, 89
    post high school plans of
        students in Green High School
        and, 94
    research integrated into, 58–62
    research options of, 55, 59–60
    rural schools committed to by, 60
    strategies of, 56–58, 130

student engagement in Green High School and, 93
student grade levels of Green High School and, 91
student identity within, 58
student involvement in leadership in Green High School and, 96
student mentoring engagement for Green High School and, 95
student reduced cost lunch participation of Green High School and, 91
training and development for, 57–58
Collins, Nick, 28, 29
community-based organizations (CBOs)
problems engaged with by, 13
strategies for education by, 5
students encouraged by, 13
Compact Scholarship, 103
Consortium on Chicago School Research, 44
Coordinate Geometry Project (CGP), 110
The Core 40, 40n1
culture, 58, 125, 126

Data-Driven Detroit, 66
data sources
action inquiry analyzing, 3
analysis of, 32
attaining of, 23
collecting of, 24–25, 35, 122, 123
DC TAG analysis of, 88
intervention identified by, 24
OSSE providing accurate, 54, 79
problems with sources of, 34
reform programs needing, 35
review of, 36
use of student, 74–75
DC Research Consortium on College Access and Retention, 49–54
DC TAG. *See* District of Columbia Tuition Assistance Grant
Department of Education, U.S., 27
Detroit
schools in, 99
Detroit Consortium, 62–68
Detroit Schools Higher Education Consortium, 40, 43, 63
Detroit Technology Academy (DTA), 110
District of Columbia's College Access Act, 52
District of Columbia's Public Education Reform Amendment Act (PERAA), 53
District of Columbia Tuition Assistance Grant (DC TAG)
cumulative graduation rate of, 80
data analysis of, 88
DC Consortium partnership with, 54
five year plan of, 54
funding for, 51–53
gender of graduates of, 79–80
graduation by high school type of, 81, 82–83
graduation rate by most attended colleges of, 86–87
graduation rate by type of first college attended of, 84–85
recipient graduation of, 79
DPS-Higher Education Consortium, 37
DTA. *See* Detroit Technology Academy

education
  actionable approach to, 7
  CBOs for, 5
  CFES and Green High School students levels of, 92
  family engagement in, 10
  inequality in, 26–29, 129
  opportunities for, 4–5, 6–7, 15
  pipeline model of, 20–21
  research standards in, 59
  transitions in, 12
education systems
  accountability in, 23
  rapid change of, 13–14
  social justice in, 119–20
emergency financial manager (EFM), 63
engaged research
  action inquiry, learning and, 69–70, 129
  case studies illustrating, 15–16
  CFES supporting, 60
  in colleges and universities, 124–27
  evaluation, organization and, 64–65
  tasks for, 74
engaged scholarship
  exchange encouraged through, 69
  opportunity expanded by, 69
  pathways interpreted by, 119, 127
  practice refined by, 127–28
  resources provided by, 41
  standard of, 47
  strategies tested by, 1, 4
  as teacher strategy, 1
equity, 1, 19
ESD. *See* Excellent Schools Detroit
ethnicity, 92
evaluation

action inquiry, research and, 73–74, 76
  in action inquiry cycle, 46
  boundaries of, 74
  designs for, 73
  as first step, 44–45
  intervention included in, 43, 45–46
  organization, engaged research and, 64–65
  system review of, 31
Excellent Schools Detroit, 66
experience
  learning from, 3, 18, 119
  reflection on personal, 16–17
external reporting, 32

FAFSA. *See* Free Application for Federal Student Aid
Ford Foundation, 15, 64, 65, 67
Free Application for Federal Student Aid (FAFSA), 54
funding
  agencies for, 48
  for CFES, 29–30
  for DC TAG, 51–52
  from Ford Foundation, 64
  as per-student, 38
  for researchers, 24, 109
  research obtaining, 48
  students needing, 18–19

Green High School
  ethnicity of students of CFES and, 92
  mentoring engagement for students in CFES and, 95
  post high school plans of students in CFES and, 94
  student education levels of CFES and, 92

student engagement in CFES and, 93
student grade levels of CFES and, 91
student involvement in leadership in CFES and, 96
student reduced cost lunch participation of CFES and, 91
student survey of, 90–96

High School Summer Program Incorporating Urban Debate League, 67
hypotheses, refining of, 25

Indiana Project on Academic Success (IPAS), 43
inequality
 in education, 26–29, 129
 interventions on, 37
 issues with, 19
 key indicators of, 24
 organization promoting, 42
 reducing of, 42–43
 in United States, 129
information on analysis
 action informed, 74
 change using, 69
 existing, used, 25
 review of, 31–36
 sources identified of, 23
 systems generating, 18
interventions
 actionable theory tested through, 1
 challenges aligned with, 25
 change identifying, 7–8
 data sources identifying, 24
 defining of, 2
 evaluation included in, 43, 45–46

on inequality, 37
perspectives utilized for strategies of, 78
research on, 32, 46–47
resources utilized by, 2
strategies for, 2, 3
students empowered by, 11

Ladies of Distinction, 99–100, 102, 107
leadership
 in action inquiry groups, 125
 Green High School and CFES student involvement in, 96
 OSSE change in, 53
 through service, 95–97
learning for change
 action inquiry, engaged research and, 69–70, 129
 teachers orientation of, 14
literacy reform, 28
Loyola High School Program Developing College Knowledge, 67

math reform, 28, 109
MBLT. *See* More and Better Learning Time
Meares, Henry, 63–64
memo of understanding, 122
memorandum of understanding (MOU), 65
mentoring programs
 accountability learned through, 104–5
 CFES and, 56
 challenges in, 106–7
 college-going culture promoted by, 102
 community exposure in, 105
 emergent themes in, 100

engagement in, for students, 95
field trips within, 105
improvement for, 107
student confidence gained through, 99, 101, 102, 104
tutoring and, 99
mentorship, 103–5
Michigan Merit Exam, 63, 110
More and Better Learning Time (MBLT), 66
MOU. *See* memorandum of understanding

A Nation at Risk (Department of Education, U.S., 1983), 27
networks
gaps in support, 12
identifying of, 12
organization of local, 49
student success supported by, 10–12
9-14 system
transition to, 20
Norton, Eleanor Holmes, 52

Office of the State Superintendent of Education (OSSE), 49, 50, 52
data provided by, 54, 79
leadership change at, 53
PERAA and, 53
organization
CFES process of, 57
equity promoted by, 42
evaluation, engaged research and, 64–65
of local networks, 49
partnerships approach to, 9–10
partnerships capacity for, 43
of research partnerships, 55
strategies of, 44

student centered approach to, 9–10
student opportunities expanded by, 41
OSSE. *See* Office of the State Superintendent of Education

partners
communication among, 42
researchers as, 23
strength recognized in, 41
partnerships
actionable theory assisting, 11
action inquiry building, 48–49
action knowledge generated by, 128
aligning of, 44
approach to organization in, 9–10
building of strong, 122
of CFES, 55, 56
collaboration provided by, 18, 120
contexts for creating urban, 28–29
with DC Research Consortium on College Access and Retention, 53
improvement valued in, 124
movement within, 121
opportunity expanded by, 13
organizational capacity built around, 43
organization of research, 55
patience and persistence for establishing, 121
power of dynamics in, 123
resources forming, 11
social justice promoted by, 4, 42
students empowered by, 12
trust required by, 120–21

pathways
  to college and careers, 90–91
  engaged scholarship interpreting, 119, 127
  forming of, 21
  for students, 75
  understanding of, 26
PD. *See* professional development
PERAA. *See* District of Columbia's Public Education Reform Amendment Act
poverty, as student risk factor, 39
practice
  actionable theory strategy identified by, 9
  of CFES, 30–31, 37, 58
  engaged scholarship refining, 127–28
  opportunities to improve, 14
  projects informed by, 45
  reflecting on, 6, 116
  reflections on, 6, 116
  research aligned with, 19
  student surveys informing, 77
problems
  CBOs engaging, 13
  with data sources, 34
  emerging of, 15
  in high schools, 59
  PD supporting solving of, 110
professional development (PD)
  problem solving supporting, 110
  teachers conceptualization of, 115
  teachers encouraging, 116
Projects Promoting Equity in Urban and Higher Education, 15, 49
propensity score matching (PSM), 32–34

RD. *See* regression discontinuity

reflections
  on action, 127
  on barriers, 14
  on personal experience, 16–17
  on practice, 6, 116
  questions and, 29, 37, 40, 54, 62, 68, 89, 98, 108, 118
  on research, 15
reform programs
  curriculum improved by, 27
  financial aid supported by, 27
  information informing effectiveness of, 35
  learning from, 27–28
  outreach and encouragement in, 27
  research relied on by, 34
  support services provided by, 27–28
regression discontinuity (RD), 32–34
RESA. *See* Wayne State Regional Educational Service Agency
research. *See also* engaged research
  action inquiry, evaluation and, 73–74, 76
  action inquiry, social justice and, 48, 129
  barriers identified with, 71
  change made by, 70, 125
  coordinating process of, 43
  DC Consortium agenda for, 50–52
  education standards of, 59
  funding obtained by, 48
  of intervention, 32, 46–47
  partnerships of CFES, 55, 59–60
  practice aligned with, 19
  questions on, 125–26
  reflections on, 15
  reform programs relying on, 34

revision as constant in, 126
strategic initiatives informed by, 55–58
surveys, accountability and, 98
use of, 108
vetting and releasing of, 47
Research and Action Partnership With Covenant House Academies, 67
researchers
   collaboration between teachers and, 120–21
   funding for, 24, 109
   as partners, 23
resources
   engaged scholarship providing, 41
   intervention utilizing, 2
   partnerships formed by, 11
   students success created by community, 66
Rex, Lesley, 28
robust dialogue, 27

scholarship, 69. *See also* engaged scholarship
school choice theory, 39
schools
   access to, 122–23
   achievements in old and new, 38–40
   advanced math courses in urban, 109, 111
   CFES committing to rural, 60
   challenges faced by urban, 26
   in Detroit, 99
   problems in, 59
   site visits to, 36
   student achievement in Detroit, 37
   of students of DC TAG, 81, 82–83

social context, 28
social justice
   action inquiry, research and, 48, 129
   barriers to, 2, 18
   in education systems, 119–20
   partnerships promoting, 4, 42
sources
   types of, 111, 112, 112n2, 115
STEM fields, 20–21, 117
students
   academic achievement of, 100–101
   academic preparation for, 20
   action inquiry empowering, 6–7
   barriers of underrepresented, 22
   CBOs encouraging, 13
   CFES and Green High School grade levels of, 91
   CFES and Green High School mentoring engagement for, 95
   CFES identity for, 58
   CFES serving, 30
   challenges for, 97, 117
   college interest of, 93
   data of, 74–75
   debt for, 6
   education levels of CFES and Green High School, 92
   funding needed for, 18–19, 38
   graduation requirements for, 10
   Green High School and CFES engagement of, 93
   Green High School and CFES reduced cost lunch participation of, 91
   Green High School survey of, 90–96
   high schools of DC TAG, 81, 82–83
   hope needed by, 130

intervention empowering, 11
interviews and focus groups of, 77–78
life circumstances influencing, 14
mentoring programs boosting confidence for, 99, 101, 102, 104
networks supporting success of, 10–12
organization expanding opportunities for, 41
partnerships empowering, 12
pathways formed for, 75
as peers, 104
peers identified by, 117
post high school plans of Green High School and CFES, 94
poverty as risk factor for, 39
practice informed by surveys of, 77
statistics of, 52
survey of, 35, 46, 60, 89
teachers view of, 114–15
surveys
accountability, research and, 98
development of, 77
fall and spring option for, 97–98
of Green High School students, 90–96
instruments for, 77
of program directors, 36
of students, 35, 46, 60, 77, 89, 90, 96
understanding built by, 74
use of, 75–76
as valuable, 36
systems. *See also* education systems
for accountability, 31, 77–78

change supported by, 47–48
evaluation review, 31
information generated by, 18
transition to 9-14, 20

targets, 111–12, 113, 115
teachers
challenges faced by, 62–63
collaboration between researchers and, 121–22
communication as difficult for, 113–14
as engaged, 73
interviews with, 111
issues observed by, 116
learning orientation of, 14
PD conceptualization by, 115
PD encouraged by, 116
positive contributions from, 114–15
sources and targets of issues cited by, 112, 115
students viewed by, 114–15
thought partners, 12
trust, 120–21
Twenty-First Century Scholars, 27

United Way, 66

Washington State Achievers (WSA), 27
Wayne State Regional Educational Service Agency (RESA), 66
Williams, Dawn, 51
Williams, John B., 28–29, 49
Winfrey, Tyrone, 63–64
WSA. *See* Washington State Achievers

Publicly Engaged Scholars
Next-Generation Engagement and the Future of Higher Educations
Edited by Margaret A. Post, Elaine Ward, Nicholas V. Longo, and John Saltmarsh
Foreword by Timothy K. Eatman
Afterword by Peter Levine

"*Publicly Engaged Scholars* is both unflinching in its presentation of the challenges—personal, professional, political—facing those who seek to transform higher education for the greater good and hopeful in its demonstration of the persistence and adaptability of engaged scholarship. Anyone concerned about higher education's contribution to democracy should read it."—***Andrew J. Seligsohn***, *President, Campus Compact*

Research, Actionable Knowledge, and Social Change
Reclaiming Social Responsibility Through Research Partnerships
Edward P. St. John
Foreword by Penny A. Pasque

"St. John's book offers hope for practitioners, researchers, and policymakers interested in moving past studying problems and moving toward addressing them. He provides both theoretical and practical guidance for individuals designing and engaging with actionable research. This book serves as a useful tool for graduate students, seasoned scholars, and those outside the academy who are interested in building partnerships."
—***Ronald Hallett***, *Assistant Professor, Director, Creating Opportunities Via Education, Benerd School of Education, University of the Pacific*

Sty/us

22883 Quicksilver Drive
Sterling, VA 20166-2102

Subscribe to our e-mail alerts: www.Styluspub.com

Also available from Stylus

Community-Based Research
Teaching for Community Impact
Edited by Mary Beckman and Joyce F. Long
Foreword by Timothy K. Eatman

"As a resource to assist scholars and practitioners who wish to effectively conduct [community-based research] CBR, this volume provides useful suggestions for facilitating the process and substantive examples of research projects within a range of disciplines and at different stages of development. Equally important is its potential to serve as an instrument to facilitate strategic thinking and a design for research undertakings that lead to ameliorative outcomes and impact in the communities where the work is done. As such, this book advances the field significantly and helps move us toward these purposes in a focused manner. The aims of this volume are needed to strengthen the field, but especially the second purpose—focus on CBR impact—helps us to attend to critical but often overlooked ethical issues of engagement research. This book likewise presents a powerful set of methodological choices to advance the mission and to provoke the kind of momentum needed to sustain the field."—*Timothy K. Eatman*, *Higher Education Department, School of Education, Syracuse University, and Faculty Codirector, Imagining America*

Engaging Higher Education
Purpose, Platforms, and Programs for Community Engagement
Marshall Welch
Foreword by John Saltmarsh

"Rarely in a maturing scholarly field does a volume provide both breadth and depth of scholarship on community engagement, but Marshall Welch's volume accomplishes this feat masterfully. Welch provides an overview of the community engagement field in its current state, rooted in research and scholarly analysis. From its historical origins as a movement to the evolution of community engagement as a field, this volume extends an evidence-based synthesis of how higher education systems structure and implement community engagement, as well as a 'how-to' for higher education institutions. It will serve multiple purposes for higher education administrators, faculty, community engagement center directors, and graduate students in education."
—*Patrick M. Green*, *Founding Director, Center for Experiential Learning, Loyola University Chicago; Past Board Chair, International Association for Research on Service-Learning and Community Engagement*

(Continues on previous page)